William Athenry Whyte

A Land Journey from Asia to Europe

Being an Account of a Camel and Sledge Journey From Canton to...

William Athenry Whyte

A Land Journey from Asia to Europe
Being an Account of a Camel and Sledge Journey From Canton to...

ISBN/EAN: 9783744798211

Printed in Europe, USA, Canada, Australia, Japan

Cover: Foto ©Andreas Hilbeck / pixelio.de

More available books at **www.hansebooks.com**

A LAND JOURNEY

FROM

ASIA TO EUROPE:

BEING AN ACCOUNT OF

A CAMEL AND SLEDGE JOURNEY FROM CANTON TO ST. PETERSBURG
THROUGH THE PLAINS OF MONGOLIA AND SIBERIA.

BY

WILLIAM ATHENRY WHYTE, F.R.G.S.

LONDON:
SAMPSON LOW, SON, AND MARSTON,
CROWN BUILDINGS, 188, FLEET STREET.
1871.

Dedicated

TO

MY FRIEND AND TRAVELLING COMPANION,

A. F. WALCOTT, Esq.,

OF NEW YORK.

TEDDINGTON,
April 4, 1871.

CONTENTS.

CHAPTER I.

Arrive at Hong Kong and proceed to Canton—Curious Sights in the City—The Beggars' Square — The Temples—Pawnbrokers' Towers—The Walls—The City of the Dead—The Foreign Settlements—Macao—Agree with Mr. Walcott to take the Land Journey home, through Mongolia and Siberia, the only Sea Passage being the Straits of Dover—Our Outfit —Sail for Shanghae—Arrival at Shanghae—The Foreign Concessions—Searching for drowned Chinese Boys in the English Settlement—Pusillanimous Policy of the English Government—Prosperous Condition of Shanghae—Sail for Tientsin—The Peiho River, its intricate Navigation—Dummy Forts—We arrive at Tientsin—Further Preparations for our Land Journey—We leave Tientsin in our Carts—Hostility of the Chinese—A rough Ride to Poogow—First Night in our Carts in the Yard of a Chinese Inn—We arrive at Pekin —Incivility of the British Embassy and kind Reception at the American Legation — Dreary Appearance of Pekin — Ignorance of the Literati—The Imperial City—Kindness of the Russian Embassy 1

CHAPTER II.

We start for Kalgan—The Ruins of the Summer Palace— Magnificence of the Great Wall—A Sand-storm—Nankin Pass—Deserted Fortifications—The Wind upsets my Mule Litter close to a Precipice—The Great Wall runs beside us over lofty Mountains—Descent from the Pass, and the Commencement of the Great Desert—Wun-lie-Cheong a most interesting Town—Sha-shing—A Chinaman attempts to rob me at Night—Warned off by my Revolver—Chang-chia-Kow, or Kalgan, the last Town in China Proper—The Bustle of the Streets like a Scene in the 'Arabian Nights'—The most prosperous Town of its Size in China—Lodged in the House of a Russian Merchant—Preparations for crossing the Desert of Gobi—We engage for Guides two Lama Priests, and hire Carts and Camels, and lay in all necessary Stores—Our Start on the long Desert Journey—Magnificent View from the Top of a Pass—Leave the Great Wall and enter Mongolia—Mistake of the last Chinese Treaty . 34

CHAPTER III.

The Start—In our Carts, harnessed to Camels—We shoot some Hawks, to the Astonishment of the Guides, who have never seen a repeating Rifle fired—Our first Encampment—The Desert becomes bare of Pasture—We meet the first Caravan from Kiachta—Purchase two Ponies of a Mongol Horse dealer—The Steeds turn restive—A Tussle in the Desert—Visit from an old Mongol—Hospitality of these People—Their Habits and Occupations—Sunrise in the Desert—Our Camels break down—A Mongol Venus—A Visit to one of the *Yourts*, or Tents—Bargaining for fresh Camels—Want of Water—A Mirage in the Desert—Intruders join us—Knocked up at night in my Cart by one of them asking for Liquor—Fire my Revolver in reply—My new Camel turns restive, and nearly pitches me out of my Cart—The Plain covered with Camels' Bones—The horrible Cold of a North-easter—The effect of the Atmosphere in magnifying distant Objects—Attempt to steal our Camels by mounted Mongols—We name our Mongol Lama Guides 'Monkey' and 'Cocoanut'—The Cold increasing—Our Ponies getting starved for want of Fodder—More than half frozen in my Cart: the Pain of being thawed—We reach Tsagan Tugurik—Vast Herds of

Camels—We present a Mongol with some Cayenne Pepper
to stop begging for Whisky—Signs of Ironstone and Copper
Ore 78

CHAPTER IV.

How the Mongols cure a Camel's cracked Hoof—The Tartar
Village of Wyshan—Great Dwelling-place of Lama Priests
—The Country for a Railroad from Russia to China—My
Camel becomes untied from our Train, and I am left alone
in the Night in the Desert, without Food—Cocoanut returns
and finds me—A Lot of Marmots—A Plateau surrounded
with Rocky Mountains—Herds of Ponies, Camels, and wild
Gurush—Provisions running scarce, we purchase a Sheep of
some Mongols—A Difficulty in killing him—We kill a wild
Gurush—Signs of the End of the Desert—Notwithstanding
our Hardships, our Retrospect a pleasant one—The way I
kept Time—A Storm of Sand and Stones—We visit a Yourt,
to warm ourselves—The half-breed Mongols bad Characters
—As my Head is bald I am taken for a Lama—Camels without Water for Ten Days—My Experience as to the Kind of
Cart to travel with—We descend into a deep Valley—A
Russian knocks us up at Night, a sign we were getting near
our Journey's End—The North-east Wind nearly freezes us
to our Carts—An Obon—A magnificent Prospect of Rocky
Crags at our Feet 118

CHAPTER V.

Our Provision Camel is lost, and Cocoanut goes in search of
him—The other Camels refuse to descend the steep Incline,
and the Ponies scamper off—Our remaining Guide goes to
get Water, and we have to lead the Camels and Horses—Our
remarkable Appearance in our Sheep-skin Clothing—Cocoanut and Monkey return again with the missing Camel—The
Winter the best Season to do the Journey in—Pleasures of a
free Life in the Desert—We cross the River Toll on the Ice—
We reach the Chinese town of Mai-Mai-Chin—We visit the

Russian Consulate—The Vice-Consul greets us with Delight —The only Europeans he had seen for a long time—We take leave of the Mongolian Desert here, and enter Siberia.— Russia gradually encroaching upon the whole of Mongolia— Mai-Mai-Chin, the residence of the Lama King—Account of the Lama King, and his Method of Succession—We taste the Pleasures of Civilisation once more—We sell our Ponies here and start the same Day—An unpleasant Adventure in my Cart—We start against our Lamas' Wishes—Oxen engaged to take us up the Mountain Pass—Queer Costume of the female Driver— Perils of the Descent — We continue to ascend and descend 155

CHAPTER VI.

We cross the Rivers Boro and Cara—My Cart sticks in the latter Stream—We ascend the Pass of Cara — The Hills covered with Pine Forests—Delightful Sensation of passing through these Forests after the flat Plain—Oxen procured to make the Ascent—The Top of the Pass marked by a huge Obon made of Wood and Camel's Hair—We descend into another Valley—A strange Herd of Cattle—We meet Tartars on Horseback—Their method of capturing Ponies with the Lasso—A magnificent Prospect—My Health benefited by my open-air Life notwithstanding Privations—The Country becomes more populous as we proceed—We cross the River Sha-Ragol—The Cold increases and the Camels begin to fail —Cocoanut in his Sleep nearly brings the Caravan to grief— We enter a Pine Forest—We reach a vast Plain, at the End of which appear the Spires of Kiachta . . 188

CHAPTER VII.

Kiachta—The Luxury of a Russian Bath after our Travels—We visit the Commissaire Impérial—Method of conducting the Postal Routes— Method of warming a Russian House—Festivals of the Jour de Nom—Curiosities of Costume in Russia— We meet an Englishman—A Russian Dinner—The Ladies'

CONTENTS. xiii

PAGE

Room – Russia the great Cigarette Country—The Riches of the Kiachta Merchants—The Magnificence of the Greek Church —The Chinese Town of Mai-Mai-Chin adjoining Kiachta— Signs of its Importance and Wealth—The Yamun of the Chinese Governor—We experience the Advent of Civilisation by sending a Telegram to London—An English Dinner at last—A Russian Gentleman agrees to join us in a Tarantass on our Journey to Irkoutsk—Hospitality of the Russians—Their Acquaintance with English Authors—The Bread-throwing Custom—A Description of the Town of Kiachta—Expenses of our Outfit and Postal Blanks for our future Journey—We start in our Tarantass, and arrive at Auskiachta, where our Russian travelling Companion, Col. B——, joins us—We proceed onward to Korai—Tremendous Pace of our Tarantass downhill 218

CHAPTER VIII.

We arrive at the River Selinga and cross it by the Ferry Boat The town of Selenginsk—Disgusting Condition of the Posthouse—We find a Friend—The intense Cold as we proceed to Obokunztske—The splendid State of the Snow Roads, and the Pace of our Tarantass, especially downhill—Gaps in the Road and Jumps in our Conveyance—We arrive at Sichanonar —We skirt along the Lake Baikal—Sudden Storms upon this Lake—The Splendid Scenery—We pass through fine Pine Forests—Mechia—The Site of a Battle Field between the Poles and Russians—Reports of the dismal Condition of the Roads in advance—Jumping the Sledges over Chasms in the Road—Sudden Change from Calm to a terrific Storm on the Lake 246

CHAPTER IX.

Intensity of the Cold—Horrible State of the Roads, and dangerous Situation of our Sledges—We reach Murmske—The Beauty of the Scenery at this Part of the Lake Baikal—We arrive at Mouradeofsky, and strike inland—We cross a Branch

of the River Angara, the last River to freeze in Siberia—
Irkoutsk, the capital Town of Eastern Siberia—We replenish
our Clothing and Stores—The Landlord of our Hotel attempts
to delay us—Drunkards sentenced to keep the Snow Roads
in order—We make the Acquaintance of a Russian Officer
who agrees to travel with us to St. Petersburg—Russian
Fashions with respect to Dress—Polish Exiles at Irkoutsk
—The Gold and Silver Mines of Siberia—Terrible Nature of
the Convict Labour, chiefly for political Offences—Enormous
Riches of Owners of these Mines—The Government Mines
furnish the Emperor's Income—The various Tribes in the
Neighbourhood of Lake Baikal—Different Methods of Salutation observed during our Route—A first-rate Restaurant—
—Dilatory Nature of the Town People . . 272

CHAPTER X.

The public Sledges at Irkoutsk—We kiss our male Friends and
proceed—Our Russian military Fellow-traveller is immovably wedged with us in our Sledge—We find we have been
robbed whilst at the last Hotel—We reach Bokara—The
wedging Process in the Sledge gives us all Cramp—Our
Sledge breaks down—We thaw our Noses—After travelling
through a fine Country we arrive at Coŭtoŭlikskaya—Our
Sledge takes to sliding sideways—A warm Day, only thirty-
two Degrees of Frost—Our Drag breaks as we are going
down a precipitous Part of the Road—The Churches the
only Buildings of Importance in the Towns we pass—My
Leg nearly frost-bitten on a Sack of frozen Soup—Our
covered Sledge turned into a Stalactite Cave—Alzamayskaya
—The Delights of Sledging—We are terribly bumped by
Merchandise Sledges—Splendid Country for a Railroad—*The
Eastern Land Route*—We travel on the frozen River Yenisee
The Town of Krasnoyarsk—Obliged to buy a new Sledge—
We approach the Steppes of Baraba—A fearful Snow-storm
—Method of indicating the proper Sledge Road—We take
the wrong Route—A cut-throat Peasant Host . . 292

CHAPTER XI.

A Collision with another Sledge—The Country of Windmills—
The Telegraph Wires broken by the Snow—Disgusting Con-
dition of the Peasant Post-houses— Wolves—The River
Irtish—We quit the Steppe of Baraba—Abstemiousness and
Trustworthiness of Russian Drivers — Besroucova — Our
Driver nearly takes us over a Bank—Our Russian Fellow-
traveller leaves everything behind him—A splendid Sunset
—The Country begins to improve—A Sable in view—We
reach the Top of the Pass of the Oural Mountains—The plain
white Stone that marks the Separation between Asia and
Europe—We arrive at Nijni Novgorod, and bid farewell to
our Sledges, and proceed by Rail to Moscow, and thence on
to St. Petersburg 320

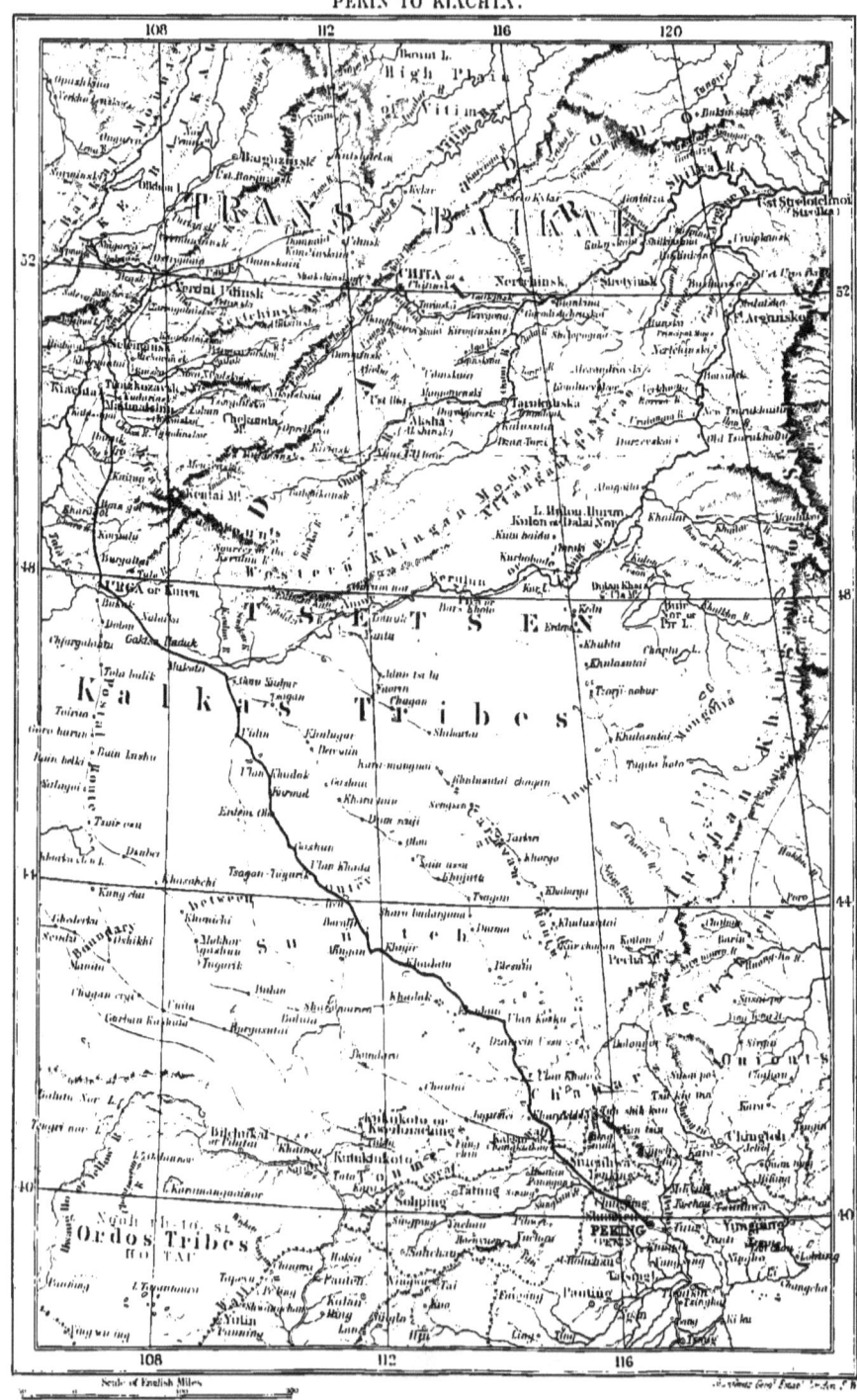

PEKIN TO KIACHTA.

A LAND JOURNEY FROM ASIA TO EUROPE.

CHAPTER I.

Arrive at Hong Kong and proceed to Canton—Curious Sights in the City—The Beggars' Square—The Temples—Pawnbrokers' Towers—The Walls—The City of the Dead—The Foreign Settlements — Macao — Agree with Mr. Walcott to take the Land Journey home, through Mongolia and Siberia, the only Sea Passage being the Straits of Dover — Our Outfit — Sail for Shanghae — Arrival at Shanghae — The Foreign Concessions — Searching for drowned Chinese Boys in the English Settlement— Pusillanimous Policy of the English Government—Prosperous Condition of Shanghae—Sail for Tientsin—The Peiho River, its intricate Navigation—Dummy Forts—We arrive at Tientsin— Further Preparations for our Land Journey—We leave Tientsin in our Carts—Hostility of the Chinese—A rough Ride to Poogow —First Night in our Carts in the Yard of a Chinese Inn—We arrive at Pekin—Incivility of the British Embassy and kind Reception at the American Legation—Dreary Appearance of Pekin —Ignorance of the Literati—The Imperial City—Kindness of the Russian Embassy.

I LEFT England by the ordinary overland route on the 1st of May, 1869, and after a very pleasant journey—that is to say, taking all the disagreeables of a sea voyage into consideration—I arrived at Hong Kong on the 16th of June, and was very glad once more to put my foot on terra firma.

I had intended making my way home again *viâ* Japan, San Francisco, and America, but subsequent events altered my plans.

Remaining a few days in Hong Kong, I took the steamer *Kiukiang* to Canton, where I intended remaining some little time, and reached that celebrated city all safely. I took up my residence with my old friend the Venerable Archdeacon Gray, who is as well known as he is respected by all European residents in China.

Canton is certainly the best city in China. Although, as may be said of all cities in the Empire, the streets are very narrow and ill-paved, still they are clean and lined with good shops, indicating great prosperity. The people are well dressed, and look well fed; in fact, there is an air of prosperity and content reigning over the whole city. Of course, as is the case in all large towns, one is apt to come across sights which revolt the senses. I should say the principal one in Canton is the "beggars' square," where I have seen some half a dozen poor wretches stretched out, barely covered by mats, hourly awaiting death to relieve them from their misery, some of them already in a state of decomposition. The Chinese have no feeling of pity in their nature, and consequently charity is very rare with them. For a foreigner such sights as the beggars' square present, are revolting, and calculated to induce pity. The Chinaman would look upon such feelings with contempt. Celestials are not given to hold out helping hands to each other. I should say they are the most selfish, superstitious, money-loving people created. To see Canton well would take many months — I mean, to understand and remember all one can see. The principal sights are the various temples, among them that of the Five Hundred Wise Men (or gods), Longevity, and the Emperor's temple; the walls, which go all round the city; the various guilds, pawnbrokers' towers, which are a great institution in China; jewellers' shops, &c. The City of the Dead is perhaps one of the most curious sights that can be seen — a city walled round and garrisoned, with streets laid out with rows of houses; the whole kept perfectly clean. In each little house I saw one or more coffins, generally of mandarins, waiting for the lucky day to be pronounced by the soothsayer ere they can be consigned to the earth. I believe some had been there twenty years waiting the favourable opportunity. The silence of the whole place as we wandered through the deserted streets was most impressive, and I could not help remarking the same, through an interpreter, to the Chinese guide who was conducting us through. "Ah," said he, "you should be here at night, and you would see a far different sight! All the spirits walk about and conduct their business as usual. Why," said he, "these streets are quite full." He said he had never seen them, but, being sure of the fact, he never ventured out of his little cottage at the gate of the city at night. I think, when he told us, he grew paler, as he firmly believed all he said. A company of Chinese troops garrison the outer walls, as otherwise gangs of robbers would carry off the coffins, and hold them for a ransom; and if there is one superstition the Chinese respect more than another it is, to bury the remains of their relatives properly; and even afterwards they make a yearly pilgrimage to see that the graves are in order and properly cared for. I have heard it said that they do it out of affection for the dead, but I believe they merely do it because they are afraid if they neglected the dead they would be visited by their spirits, and probably not make so much money as they desire.

Then there are the " old man's home " and the " old woman's home," separate villages; and very dirty ones they are. These are charities, but how kept up I do not know. Anyhow, they do not impress one with their magnificence ; the names sound very well, but the realities are very poor indeed.

If I were to attempt to give any true description of Canton and all I have seen in it, I should fill up a large space, which I have not time or energy to do. I can only say that all I saw was by the kindness of Archdeacon Gray, who, I really think, knows the city and all about it better than any of the inhabitants, and who can tell you pretty nearly at every corner some fact or fable connected with it.

The city of Canton is situated on the right bank of the noble Pearl River. Honam is on the left, and further upon the right again is the small island Shameen, the English and French settlement. Most of the merchants have their places of business in Honam, and their dwelling-houses in Shameen.

After a pleasant sojourn of three months I left Canton, paying a passing visit to the Portuguese settlement of Macao, the sanatorium of the south of China, so called, although for what reason I hardly know, as when I was there it was awfully hot. It is a great place of resort for bridal couples, also for the dwellers in Hong Kong, who cross over on Saturdays and return on Mondays, and indulge in very sumptuous breakfasts on Sundays. There is a great deal in imagination; so, no doubt, many people do fancy Macao very healthy, and consequently do not complain so much as they would in Hong Kong, which they fancy unhealthy. I should say Macao was a splendid place for eye diseases, for anything like the glare I never experienced anywhere.

The principal products of Macao are decidedly very dirty and repulsive beggars. Every other creature seems to be a beggar or a lunatic. The inhabitants are certainly not handsome, as may be expected from a mixed breed of Portuguese and Chinese. The population is mainly hybrid, at least seven-eighths of the people being of this mixed Chinese type. On first approach, Macao gives one the idea of a strongly fortified place, but on inspection one finds it to be all a grand sham. The walls, on which antiquated popguns are placed, are painted outside, being only made of plaster, &c., something like Vauxhall Gardens used in old times to exhibit. From one of the batteries a salute on one occasion was fired, and the walls crumbled away instantaneously. It looks picturesque, but is very useless.

I wonder the Chinese have never taken Macao back. I should not think it would be an enterprise of much difficulty. The scenery about Macao is beautiful. The situation of the town and the bay reminds one very much of Naples. Of course, being Portuguese, or rather Macanese, it is Roman Catholic, and, from outward appearance, most devout. Bells ringing at all hours, and half-caste looking shovel-hatted priests wandering about. All the rites of the Church are adhered to in most exaggerated form, which really reminds one very much of the sort of worship one sees in the neighbouring Chinese temple, and seems quite as incomprehensible. The trade of Macao since the cession of Hong Kong to England has nearly died away and at present is most insignificant.

A day or two at Macao, as far as sight-seeing is concerned, is quite enough ; so I bid adieu to the beautiful spot, with its dummy forts, antiquated-looking soldiers, gambling-shops, pretty boat-women, beggars, church-bells, and half-caste population, with their monkey-faces, reminding one a great deal of the monkey-house of the Zoological

Gardens, and embarked on the steamer *White Cloud*, commanded by the well-known and deservedly liked Captain Carroll, and soon found myself again in Hong Kong. I had made arrangements with Mr. Walcott, an American gentleman, whose acquaintance I had made at Canton, to meet again in Hong Kong and discuss a project we had formed of visiting the north of China, and then making our way across Mongolia to Eastern Siberia, and from thence to St. Petersburg and London; so I at once set out to see him. The more we talked over the matter the more did we incline towards the journey; and though, no doubt, there were many difficulties to encounter, chiefly from the approach of winter and those which always turn up when travelling in uncivilised parts, still, after all, the idea of travelling the whole way from China to England by land, with the exception of the small crossing from Calais to Dover, was grand, and we definitively decided upon it.

We set to work at once to procure part of our outfit, intending to complete it at Shanghae, or as opportunity occurred. We intended to take as little as possible with us, sending most of our baggage by ship to England. We purchased at Messrs. Faulker's, the well-known clock and instrument makers, barometers, thermometers, &c., to take the heights, &c.; and we laid in a good stock of flannels, &c. Various were the comments made at the club at Hong Kong, and various were the cocktails we drank—at least I did—discussing the matter with our friends before starting.

But at last we said good-bye to Hong Kong, and bowled away, at several knots per hour, in the steamship *Suwonada*, on the 25th of September, for Shanghae; and I must say that I felt a sort of relief that we had made a start, although, as we got more at sea, and the wind, as it always seems to do when I unhappily find myself on the ocean, began to blow hard, my feelings were most uncomfortable; so that, beyond knowing that we duly passed Amoy and the mouth of the Foochow River, although at some distance, and that the coast of China is rocky and dangerous, very bold but quite bare, which facts, I am sorry to say, at that time I did not care a rap about, I remained tolerably torpid in my cabin. However, on the 26th, as it was tolerably smooth, although a strong northeaster was blowing, I managed to find my sea legs again and keep them; although on the 27th it blew tremendously, and demonstrated the fact that the steamship *Suwonada* was a very lively ship indeed, as well as being so very comfortable. Having nothing to do beyond walking up and down the deck, which, besides being very monotonous, became an operation of some difficulty on account of the pitching of the ship, I overhauled my outfit, and found it to consist of one dozen flannel shirts, some thick socks and stockings, thick underclothes, very thick short coat, revolver, thirteen-repeating rifle, and small medicine-chest. Of course I increased the outfit at Shanghae, but we both found that we could have done with less than we took, as, when in Siberia, we were able to procure furs, which are most necessary. The only fault we made was in not taking enough wine and spirits.

On the 28th and 29th we had to steam against a tremendous north-east wind, keeping out about three miles from shore, and on the 30th, much to my delight, we entered the Shanghae River, and reached the bar at Woosung at 8 A.M., but just missed the tide; so we had to remain at anchor until 5 P.M., when we were enabled to cross and proceed to Shanghae, which place we reached at half-past six in the evening, and were met by Messrs. Oliphant and Co.'s boat, at whose residence we received a most hospitable welcome, for which I know I was most sincerely grateful.

I did feel so happy to be on shore again, as we had experienced a good deal of pitching and tossing during the five days of our trip, and besides, I had suffered a great deal from rheumatism. The distance from Hong Kong to Shanghae, I believe, is about 820 miles. Having suffered so much from rheumatism, I felt great misgivings as to my being able to go on with the proposed journey; but when I thought of the miseries of being at sea, which I should have to endure by going home the ordinary route, I felt decidedly inclined to risk it; and when I woke up next morning, after a good night's rest, feeling much better, my mind remained unaltered.

It was cold after Hong Kong, the thermometer standing at 62° at mid-day. Foreign residents were making ready for the winter, which is sometimes very severe: a fact which makes Shanghae very trying, as the heat in the summer is also most intense, and consequently both extremes are very much felt. The country round Shanghae is most uninteresting, being very flat. The banks of the river are muddy and swampy, and consequently fever and ague are very prevalent at certain seasons.

The foreign "concessions" are situated on the right bank of the river. The first, approached from Wosung, is the American, occupied chiefly by wharves, warehouses, and grog shops. Then comes the English, divided from the American by the Soochow Creek. This is occupied by English and American merchants chiefly, and it presents a very fine appearance on the river. Splendid stone houses extend some distance, and in front of them a fine parade, or bund, faced with stone, and opposite the English consulate some small but pretty public gardens are planted. The French concession follows, divided also from the English by a small creek. Properly speaking there is only one concession, viz., the French one, taken by force; the others are settlements granted by the Chinese.

A very curious thing happened while we were at Shanghae, in connection with the new English church, which stands in the English settlement and is a very handsome building. A sort of idea had been promulgated, doubtless by the mandarins, who are generally at the bottom of all the ill-feeling excited against foreigners, that in order to propitiate the evil spirits supposed to be feared by the foreign residents six China boys and six girls had been buried in the small pond in front of the church. In order to disperse these rumours the trustees had the pond pumped out, and an excited crowd assembled, expecting to see the bodies. Of course none were found; had, however, some one amongst the literati or mandarins had a body secretly thrown in, the results would have been, no doubt, a rising amongst the Chinese and a general massacre, similar to the recent one in Tientsin. The excitement lasted some days, and was only allayed by representations made to the Chinese authorities. At that time all the foreign residents expected a serious row with China, sooner or later, and entirely brought on by the wretched mean policy of the English government, which allows its own subjects to be murdered with impunity. I do not believe that any consul, naval, or military officer, would dare defend his own countrymen, after the iniquitous manner in which poor Mr. Gibson was treated for doing his duty. That all the murders lately perpetrated at Tientsin are due to the present English government nobody in China can doubt. Chinamen themselves think so. The Chinese, when they see that they can murder Englishmen with impunity and evade every treaty, grow bold and aggressive, under the impression that England is no longer a power able to protect her subjects, or is afraid to do so; and there is no doubt, under the present guidance of English affairs, the whole community in China might be murdered, and it would not excite the smallest pity or action.

I was much struck with the evident signs of prosperity derived from the commercial influence, which is more marked than in any other port in China; but, at the same time, I was equally struck with the absence of all protection afforded to so large a commerce, chiefly English, by the English government. The river was full of large merchant ships, trading from all parts of the globe, and discharging their cargoes from England, America, and other countries The style of living in Shanghae is more luxurious than in other ports in China, and one cannot help being impressed with the abundant signs of wealth which are everywhere apparent, as much amongst the Chinese as the Europeans. The traveller, with a few introductory letters to European firms, always meets with the most profuse hospitality. On Sunday, the 3rd, I visited the church, which, outwardly and inwardly, is a credit to the foreign community; afterwards went with a friend to his bungalow, situated a short distance from Shanghae, and saw one of the prettiest gardens in China. What with dinners, breakfasts, and the hospitality we received from our kind American hosts, Messrs. Oliphant and Co., time soon sped on. We also replenished our stock of clothes, and laid in a store of provisions, liquors, and utensils, which were to last us as far as Kiachta. We also arranged our money matters by taking drafts on Tientsin, trusting to further arrangements from thence. We were to leave per steamer *Chili*, on the 6th, so on that morning we rose early, and packed up our various parcels, so as to have everything handy and ready for the long journey before us, and this required a deal of thought and arrangement. My packages consisted of three leathern bags, one matted package containing saddle, &c., and another containing mattress, blankets, rugs, wrappers, and a gun case. Boxes or trunks cannot be taken, as they do not fit the camels' backs so well as bags (long canvas ship's bags are the best), nor do they pack so well in sledges.

To make all sure we sent all our luggage on board the *Chili* at 6 p.m., as she was to start at daybreak on the 7th. Feeling quite easy now that the packing was over and baggage despatched, we much enjoyed dinner and the society of a few friends who were invited to meet us; and a most pleasant evening we passed, consuming, however, rather a larger quantity of whisky than we should have done on ordinary occasions in farewell toasts. It struck me several times that we ought to make a move, although I felt no uneasiness, as the *Chili* was to start at daybreak. At last, at 2.15 A.M., a small pony phaeton, something like a miniature dog-cart, came for us; one of the party on seating himself and taking the reins, enjoyed a quiet drive by himself, the pony taking him some distance before allowing himself to be pulled up. On his return, we took our places and proceeded, four of us, and the Chinese horseboy, at a good pace towards the wharf, taking the corners in fine style; it being however, for the back seats, rather difficult to avoid being shot out at sudden turnings. We reached the wharf at 2.30, but on the way I thought I could just perceive, dimly through the darkness, the outline of a large steamer slowly gliding away, and an ominous foreboding came over me that it was our steamer. However, it certainly was not daybreak. When we arrived at our destination we asked the Chinese watchman at the end of the then closed wharf, where the *Chili* was, who informed us in an injured tone, doubtless thinking what idiots we were, "The *Chili* have walkee." This was a pleasant position to be in: all our baggage gone on unaddressed, and probably no other steamer for some time. However, there was no use crying over what we could not cure. It was annoying, however, to find that the steamer had only left a few minutes, and certainly we were told she would leave at daylight.

It is generally supposed that Shanghae folks are much in advance of the age; but we never imagined to such an extent as to advance daybreak two hours. Luckily we had with us a bag containing change for a few days, so we felt not absolutely destitute. We returned home again looking and feeling rather foolish, and retired to bed, where I remained, induced by the whisky over-night, until late next morning. I could hardly realise the true state of things when I rose on the 7th, but the sight of the small supply of clothes I had soon convinced me.

We met with smiling condolences from our friends, who seemed to enjoy the joke much better than we did.

However, there we were, and no steamer advertised, so we comforted ourselves with the reflection that probably the *Chili* would have bad weather, which curiously we found afterwards was the case. The passage money from Shanghae to Tientsin is about fifteen pounds.

We passed our time in visits to the cricket-ground and bowling-alley, whose members were practising, so as to give H.R.H. the Duke of Edinburgh, expected shortly, a good game.

The 9th we were much cheered, as we were getting anxious to get on, as the season was getting late, to hear that the steamer *Shansee* would sail on the 12th, so immediately booked our berths; and on that day, after another hearty farewell, we bid our kind hosts adieu, and getting on board early this time, sailed the next morning.

It was with much regret that, on the 13th of October, we sailed away on board the steamer *Shansee* for Tientsin, having so much enjoyed our short stay at Shanghae.

It was still warm weather, the thermometer averaging 86° at noon in the shade.

As far as the Shangtung promontory, 1700 feet above the sea level, there was nothing in the coast worthy of attention; from here, however, we skirted along a fine bold coast as far as Cheefoo, 511 miles from Shanghae, which place we reached on the 14th. We found some men-of-war waiting here for the Duke of Edinburgh, who was then in Pekin. The entrance to Cheefoo is very fine. Small islands on each side and hilly country; it reminded me much of the south coast of Italy. We left again at 1 o'clock, and steamed past some very beautiful scenery for two or three miles, passing afterwards through a group of islands and across the Gulf of Petchelee, the sea being here, which is not often the case, like glass. On the 15th there were strong indications of a north-easter. About 11 A.M. we took in a pilot to cross the bar, which we must get over before entering the River Peiho. The first attempt we made was a failure, we stuck hard in the mud, and began to be afraid that we should not succeed, and so have to wait for another twenty-four hours, which, as it was now blowing, seemed no pleasant prospect. We were drawing 12 ft. and the water on the bar hardly at best tides shows so much. We had to back out of the mud and make another attempt, which, after a good deal of dragging, we happily succeeded in accomplishing.

We could now, at some distance, discern the village of Taku, and what seemed, at each side of the river, formidable forts; but on approaching nearer we found that they were only made of mud, and not all so strong as they looked in the distance. After discharging our pilot at the Chinese customhouse, a short way up the river, we proceeded as far as Cocu—twenty miles. Up to this distance the navigation is easy, but here a quantity of junks anchored in the centre, and a bend in the river like the letter S, greatly impeded us. At times a whole fleet of junks persist in anchoring at this spot, in defiance of all rules, and the crews throw stones and even fire into steamers passing. The authorities have been applied to, but with the usual result in China, they having little or no power over the owners of the junks. I believe when Admiral Keppel last went up the river in a gun-boat, the Duke of Edinburgh being on board, great difficulty was experienced in passing this spot, and that the Admiral intimated that if he found the same state of things on his return, the junks had better look out for themselves. The banks of the river are flat and uninteresting, lined with large heaps of salt, which look like small pyramids of earth, and here and there a mud village. We passed, after Cocu, through a continuation of most extraordinary bends, which puzzled me how the steamer could get round them. Once we steamed high and dry into a cabbage-garden, much to the disgust of its Celestial owner, who, while vociferating, was nearly dragged into the river by the steamer suddenly backing off and pulling the part of the bank upon which he was standing into the water. At some places we had to fasten a rope from the steamer to posts on shore, and haul round. About half-way we met H.M.S. *Salamis* (the Duke of Edinburgh on board) coming down from Tientsin. Certainly the navigation of the Peiho, as a glance at the map will show, is most intricate. Small sailing ships do manage to get up to Tientsin, but it is a long and difficult job. The bends, after passing Cocu, are most difficult to get round. There is a strong tide. About the middle of November the river becomes frozen, and is open again generally in April. There is nothing interesting beyond the well-known Peiho forts, on seeing which one can well understand how the disasters occurred during the late war.

We reached Tientsin at 6 P.M. on the 15th, and immediately set to work to make all arrangements for starting as early as possible the next day for Pekin. The first thing to do was to procure a Chinese passport, which, however, was not demanded until we reached Kiachta, and then only for our Mongol guides. This I procured through Her Majesty's consul. We then hired two servants, who spoke Pidgin English, to go with us as far as Kalgan, agreeing to pay them each at the rate of fifteen dollars per month, and if they gave satisfaction a present also. Two springless carts were next procured, and with mules and guides and plenty of provisions our arrangements were completed as far as Pekin. The Russian consul kindly gave us letters to the Russian minister in Pekin, and also to merchants in Kalgan, and very useful we found them. At Kalgan we also procured letters of credit on merchants instead of loading ourselves with Sycee silver, only taking enough to last us as far as that place.

I found that a few hours in Tientsin sufficed to see everything, there really not being anything at all of interest. The city is dirty, as all are in China, but this one probably carries the palm. The natives do not compare with those of the south. The country all round is flat and muddy. The English settlement is the only thing worth seeing, and with its front on the river looks well as it is approached; but after the other Chinese ports there is a forsaken quiet air about it, and certainly it did not impress me with an idea of prosperity.

The English consulate is about the best building in the settlement. If I were sentenced to perpetual banishment, I should look upon being sent to Tientsin as an aggravation of my sentence. I experienced very much kindness here from Mr. Moore, an American gentleman, agent of the river steamers, and it was by his assistance that we made all our arrangements for departure so promptly and so satisfactorily.

We left Tientsin at 3 P.M., on the 16th of October, 1869, in four carts, one for each of us, one for the boys, and one for our baggage. We took also two ponies, which we intended riding about twenty miles, and then sending back. We had mattresses in our carts, pillows, and some bundles of rugs, which we found very necessary, especially the latter, as the carts had no springs, and the roads were all the way abominable. I shall never forget the drive to Pekin and the dust. The carts resembled large bandboxes on wheels.

It was some time before we got clear of the long, dirty, straggling town of Tientsin. The dirt and filth, the wretched appearance of the streets, and the unsafe appearance of several wooden bridges we passed over, gave evident signs of a wretched government or of great poverty. Here and there, however, standing out from the wretchedness around, we noticed the substantial residences of the Chinese merchants. The appearance of the people indicated hostility to foreigners, as they never attempted to make way for us with the civility we had been accustomed to in the south of China, but regarded us with scowls, and made remarks, which, as we were unacquainted with the Chinese tongue, we failed to understand. That the evil feeling towards foreigners, steadily fanned into flame by the authorities, was increasing, was a notorious fact; and a war with China, brought on by the selfish policy of the English government, was imminent, any one could foresee. But, as I have before said, warnings are only pooh-pooh'd by the wise men at home, and I think we shall soon see the consequences.

It is possible to go by water to within about twenty miles of Pekin, but it takes three or four days; whereas the land transit is generally accomplished in forty-eight hours, which allows a halt for the night half way; we, however, did it in twenty-four. We paid for our carts six dollars each, half paid in Tientsin, the balance on our arrival at Pekin.

We reached Poogow at 8 o'clock, after a very rough ride, and I was very tired, and glad to dismount, as the saddle was very knobby. We dined in a Chinese hotel, using our own food, which the captain of the *Shansee* had so kindly given us. It was a novel life to us, and thinking over it now, I am glad it was last year instead of the present one, as we were entirely at the mercy of the natives. Our carts and mules stood in the centre of a large courtyard, and we were seated in a small room whose furniture consisted of a table and two wooden stools; the moon shone with the most intense brightness, and a scene of indescribable bustle and confusion and shouting presenting itself, we felt rather bewildered. We were also under the necessity of keeping an eye on our baggage cart, as several Celestials, induced by curiosity and the hope of finding something small to steal, were loafing about in a suspicious manner. We were on our way again at 11 A.M. I bolstered myself up as well as I could and tried to go to sleep, but that was simply impossible, for no sooner did I get into a comfortable position than I was jerked out of it; my bones were perfectly sore, and my head nearly broken with its constant contact with the cart. Fancy such roads approaching a capital town! On the 17th, at 5 A.M., we reached Ho-shee-wo, or "half-way place," and there we had a mild breakfast, consisting of bread and porter, and stretched our legs. We both felt bruised all over.

We were off again at 6½ A.M., and as we proceeded the roads became worse and the dust intolerable. The country we were passing through was most uninteresting,.being quite flat and very barren; only a tree here and there, and patches of Indian corn. The villages, which were few and far between, are made of mud. The people look wretchedly poor and perfectly uncivilised, but they do not mob a foreigner, as their brethren in the south did. At 12.30 A.M. we made Nea-Wan; here we dined, and were nearly dead with the shaking we had gone through. We left again at 2 P.M., and pushed on at a trot to Pekin, being afraid of arriving late, as the gates close at sunset.

Never shall I forget this latter portion of the journey: going at a trot over the most awful road, full of holes and deep in dust; and I felt I could have cried with exhaustion and the continual bumping I got. A few more miles of such torture and I should have given in or gone mad. Mouth, nose, and eyes were also choked with dust. The approach to Pekin looked most dismal, with the exception of the walls, which seemed in good repair. We just arrived in time as the gates were closing, and entered the city, and found the roads were as bad inside as outside. My friend Mr. Walcott proceeded to the American embassy, which he very much wanted me to do also; but, being a British subject, I thought it better to go to the British embassy, especially as I knew there was plenty of room there. Arriving as I did at 9 P.M., half starved, and feeling most miserable, I certainly did look forward to obtaining a shelter; but the official who received me, after casting a contemptuous glance at my wretched appearance, refused to allow me even the shelter generally accorded to a dog, and turned me out in the street, where I might have been starved or had my throat cut. He certainly did advise me to go to a Chinese hotel, but where to find one was to me uncertain, and when found I fear it would hardly have been better than sleeping in the streets. The Duke of Edinburgh having only shortly left Pekin with a large staff, there must have been plenty of room, and all I wanted was shelter for one night. With some difficulty I directed my driver to take me to the American legation, where the American acting minister, although his home was quite full, received me with much kindness, giving me one of his own rooms. My friend Walcott generously abstained from laughing at me, although he had warned me against expecting any kind of hospitality from the English legation; which, however, I was not willing to admit at the time, but I now felt very crestfallen and foolish. Considering that we all pay taxes to support these legations, I certainly can't see their object. They certainly do not protect British subjects or interests, as they do not conceal their contempt for their own countrymen. One would fancy, to see the embassy at Pekin, that its members were Chinese subjects, as they ape the style of the mandarins and servilely adore the court. I believe the English traveller's chief difficulties arise from the absurd obstructions put in his way by British officials, simply to show authority; and he need never expect hospitality from them for he will not get it. All the help and kindness I received was from Americans, officially and otherwise, who seem to take a pleasure in helping travellers on, and not obstructing them. They seem to have a sort of fellow-feeling, instead of being wrapped up in lofty officialism. I believe disturbances in China very often occur by the Chinamen seeing the contempt with which the British authorities treat their own countrymen, and they are consequently induced to do the same.

If I, as an Englishman, were invited by a mandarin to his house, the English consul, if he heard of it, would forbid me to go, and by such means the two nations are prevented from understanding one another. The consul tells his government, in excuse, that by allowing a British subject to visit freely amongst the mandarins offence is given; while the truth is the official puts an impediment in the way simply to keep up, in the mandarin's eyes, a vast distinction between himself and his countrymen.

An American finds no obstruction in his path. I often wished that for the time I could have become one.

I enjoyed the sound sleep I got, and I woke up next morning feeling quite recovered, although still much bruised. The distance from Tientsin to Pekin, I forgot to mention before, is seventy-six miles.

Pekin is now too well known for me to say much about it, but I certainly must describe my impression respecting its appearance. It is a most dreary melancholy place, and seems quite forsaken and dead, and certainly does not compare with Canton. There are some very fine buildings dispersed about, and amongst them the Temple of

Heaven, but they are all now in decay, and rapidly going to entire ruin. If China had an appropriate motto it would certainly be the word Decay!

When I read an account of my journey before the Royal Geographical Society, I stated that Pekin was, without exception, the most miserable, dirty, poverty-stricken town in China, and when that is said it means in the world. Dr. Lockhart, a well-known traveller in China, disagreed with me, and mentioned the literature of China and her productions, &c., as a proof that China was still a great nation; but I think he forgot that China has stood still for centuries, and that what used to be considered great and civilised has been passed and excelled.

To talk of Chinese literature, with the exception of the works of Confucius, is ridiculous, whilst Chinese scholars are the most ignorant fanatical set in the country, and its universities are mere shams.

I remember seeing in Canton a military examination. A deep trench was dug in a circle, and two targets were placed at equal distances from the centre. The competitor mounted a very slow pony, who trotted round the trench; the rider then approached the target, and, when close, put the arrow against it, pulled the bow, and of course each time placed the arrow successfully in the target. Three times did he perform this wondrous feat, and then, kneeling at the governor's feet, was dubbed an officer. It was so ridiculous I could hardly believe it to be true. A number of English schoolboys transported to the spot, would have died of laughter.

I have also seen the literati passing examinations, and a very dirty repulsive lot they looked. Each student has a separate cell, in which he answers set questions quietly from a crib. How any one can talk about China containing an educated race of men I cannot understand. It cannot be denied that centuries ago, even when our forefathers indulged in paint instead of garments, they were a wonderful people, and possessed for that time wonderful buildings and institutions; but they have stood still, and civilisation has left them behind, and all one finds now is decay and dilapidation. That China is rotten to the core, Pekin is now proof enough. The roads are all sand and black mud, which in rainy weather become knee deep. It cannot help striking the traveller what a miserable government the Chinese must be to permit such filth and such abject misery, which, unless seen, could scarcely be imagined. The people are like animals in their habits, without any decency whatever. They are taxed to the utmost to supply the Imperial comforts, and purposely kept in ignorance in order to ensure their submission. In the Chinese city there is scarcely a decent looking house; they seem to consist mostly of old clothes shops, made of old rags and matting, where auctions take place; here and there remnants of what might have been a fine building, but now in ruins. Such a miserable and truly God-forsaken place I never wish to see again. We both felt a relief to leave Pekin behind us. The whole place is like an ugly dream, and one can hardly repress the indignant feelings which arise when we think of the false representations English officials in China make to the government and public at home, and thus help to strengthen such a really fearful government as the Chinese, and thereby keep hundreds of thousands of fellow-creatures in disgraceful ignorance, misery, and vice. Surely retribution will some day come. There is a very fine old marble bridge—which will also in course of time be destroyed—from whence a view is obtained into the Imperial Gardens, and a very fine view it is.

The imperial city is all walled round, and

foreigners cannot obtain admission. It contrasts, as far as can be seen from the outside, very favourably with the Chinese city. There is also a fine observatory worth seeing, and last, but not least, the walls, which are really splendid, in some places seventy feet wide.

From the Russian embassy we received great kindness, and through the assistance we obtained there we got our travelling arrangements completed to Kalgan. It certainly did seem curious that an Englishman should have to find shelter at the American embassy, and have all travelling arrangements completed at the Russian, when his own embassy, the largest in the place, steadily shut its doors against him.

I mentioned it at both embassies, and neither seemed astonished, as, unless the luckless personage happens to be a somebody with a title, I was informed it was the rule laid down at the English embassy.

We laid in a few furs at Pekin, and after having spent three days, during which time we had learnt what dirt means, and also mud, we retired to rest on the 19th, looking forward to an early start next morning.

CHAPTER II.

We start for Kalgan—The Ruins of the Summer Palace—Magnificence of the Great Wall—A Sand-storm—Nankin Pass—Deserted Fortifications — The Wind upsets my Mule Litter close to a Precipice—The Great Wall runs beside us over lofty Mountains —Descent from the Pass, and the Commencement of the Great Desert—Wun-lie-Cheong a most interesting town—Sha-Shing—A Chinaman attempts to rob me at Night—Warned off by my Revolver—Chang-chia-Kow, or Kalgan, the last Town in China Proper —The Bustle of the Streets like a Scene in the 'Arabian Nights'— The most prosperous Town of its Size in China—Lodged in the House of a Russian Merchant — Preparations for crossing the Desert of Gobi—We engage for Guides two Lama Priests, and hire Carts and Camels, and lay in all necessary Stores—Our Start on the long Desert Journey—Magnificent View from the Top of a Pass—Leave the Great Wall and enter Mongolia—Mistake of the last Chinese Treaty.

WE left Pekin on the morning of the 20th of October, 1869, at 8 A.M. It was a fine clear day, but blowing hard from the north-east, which we felt very much after the great heat of the south. We were fortunately, however, provided with wraps, which made us somewhat comfortable. Our mode of travelling was in mule litters—a sort of sedan chair, not very comfortable, being only about five feet long, carried by mules on bamboos. The motion is easy, but it is very difficult to climb into or descend from them. Each time that we stopped the chairs had to be hoisted off the backs of the mules, which gives one a very unpleasant idea of being capsized—an accident which indeed did happen to me at one of the stations. The pace at which we proceeded was about three miles per hour; and partly walking and partly riding in our chairs, skirting along the magnificent outer walls of Pekin, we arrived at a small village at 1 P.M., about a mile and a half south of the imperial territory grounds of Yuen-Ming-Yuen. Here we lunched off provisions we had taken with us from Pekin. I would strongly advise travellers along this route to provide themselves with plenty of provisions, as the Chinese *cuisine* is not tempting, even when one is very hungry. Only halting here a short time, we soon made Yuen-Ming-Yuen. The scenery here is beautiful, especially after the flat and dreary plains about Pekin. The park itself is very much neglected. The temples, which must have been splendid, and the walls surrounding it, are in ruins, having been destroyed during the last Chinese war. At the entrance gate, which is now walled up, are two magnificent bronze lions, perfectly polished. As works of art they probably stand unequalled. We got through the walls, climbing over a gap; but as our time was limited, we did not see much to reward our exertions.

Formerly this park was open to foreigners, but not long since some person, an Englishman, I believe, visiting the grounds, shot a deer; in consequence, they have been closed against all visitors. It is much to be regretted that travellers so often outrage the laws and customs of the countries they pass through.

From the Yuen-Ming-Yuen we could see the ruins of the far-famed Summer Palace, which was almost entirely destroyed during the last Chinese war. This palace was formerly the summer residence of the emperors of China, and before it was burnt contained a very fine collection of antique curios, now dispersed over the world. Nothing has been done towards rebuilding it, and it stands a melancholy example of the devastating influence of war.

The whole neighbourhood teems with the ruins of what formerly were temples, palaces, and villages. The road we had passed over from Pekin to Yuen-Ming-Yuen is made of solid slabs of granite, each slab fully ten feet long, but is now, as everything else in the north of China, going to decay through neglect. What struck me as most curious was the quantity of walls we saw, every building being surrounded by a strong wall, of course now in decay, and some even have two or three round them. As for the walls of Pekin, it seemed as if we never should get away from them, so great in extent are they. Our route now lay in a north-westerly direction. As we proceeded onwards, the character of the country changed, from the flat plains which had wearied us so long, to rocky and mountainous scenery; but trees got more scarce, and cultivation disappeared rapidly, none of the plants or exotics which are so abundant in the south being found here.

We passed the night at Quang-Shee, and were glad to get any shelter, as the wind had increased considerably, and threatened at times to overthrow our litters. Entering the court of the Chinese hotel, which was as destitute of comfort as any we had seen before, but decidedly cleaner, we were hoisted off our mules, and, after seeing our baggage safely stowed away, retired to rest. The distance we had made during the day was twenty-seven miles, or eighty-one *li*.

At 7 A.M. the next day, we were all again ready for a start, the wind blowing as hard as ever, and the thermometer standing at 42° Fahrenheit.

Having paid our bill at the hotel, which did not amount to much, we resumed our journey, and commenced a most disagreeable ride over a sandy plain, where we were nearly smothered with sand and small stones raised by the wind, which penetrated into our clothes, mouth, eyes, and even into our boxes of provisions, rendering us perfectly miserable for a time, and raising in me doubts of my capability of crossing the desert of Mongolia. However, every misery has an end some time or other, and the slightest alleviation seems perfect happiness. There is nothing like going through a sand-storm driving in one's face for three hours to make one appreciate the shelter even of a Chinese hotel, and we never felt more happy than when we entered the courtyard of the hotel at the town of Nankow, situated at the foot of the Nankow Pass. We stopped there for one hour, to give our mules a rest, as going through the pass, or rather defile, is very serious work. Our direction was now more westerly. The pass is entered through a defile of high mountains, surrounded with fortifications in all directions, now fallen out of use, and consequently going to decay. They were originally built against the Tartars. A small disciplined army would easily defy the forces of barbaric intruders. The road, which still shows a few signs of having been regularly made, is now in a state of nature, and was about the worst and roughest we passed over.

It would be impossible for any conveyance with wheels to pass over it, the only method being with camels or mule litters. I mention this because we had been told that it was possible to travel from Pekin to Chang-chia-Kow with carts. My mules had two or three times nearly landed me over a precipice, struggling along over the slippery stones, and it is a wonder to me how they did manage to get on at all, at every turn meeting a violent gust of wind which nearly blew the litter over. I therefore decided to walk, so toiled along over rocks and stones, across streams, &c., and found it as rough a walk as the most enthusiastic Alpine traveller could desire. The rise is very gradual, the whole length of the pass being rather over thirteen miles. Here we lost all signs of verdure of any kind, and from henceforward, for an indefinite period, trees ceased to form a feature in the landscape we passed through. About half-way through the pass we came to a very quaint old arch; it was impossible to distinguish any date, but it was covered with carved Indian figures. How it got there is a mystery. Here I began to feel tired, not being yet much accustomed to walking, so climbed again into my litter. However, I had not proceeded far when, just as we were passing over a very ticklish place, a tremendous gust of wind caught my litter and blew it right over. Luckily for me, between the litter and a precipice of 700 feet or more there was a rock, and on this it hung; but being only suspended on the mules' backs, I might easily have gone over. To make matters worse, one of the mules commenced kicking, and as I could not get out, and was within a few inches of his feet, my position was anything but comfortable, especially as I expected every minute to see the litter, which was only made of bamboo, part in two. By dint of great exertion and a great deal of shouting, which, being in Chinese, we did not understand, I was at last extricated. My travelling companion, who saw me go over, could do nothing, as his mules stopped in a most awkward place, and he was afraid of moving for fear of going over himself. After it was over we could not help laughing at the helpless condition we had been in, at the same time fully agreeing that it had also been very dangerous. My fellow-traveller's fear had been lest his mules should advance, in which case he would probably have lost his balance, as the guides were both with me, busily employed in shouting, which is always a Chinaman's idea of getting out of a scrape; and I might well have been at the bottom of the precipice while they were still arguing as to the best method of extricating me from the litter. One soon loses sight and remembrance of danger in the contemplation of the glorious scenery nature affords us, especially in this part of the world, and as the ruddy tints of the descending sun cast its reflection on the mountain tops and coloured all around with its magnificence, our thoughts were soon diverted, and we could not help feeling it was worth while even risking one's life to see such a sight. Imagine as wild a spot as nature can afford, all around lofty mountains, and up their crests gigantic walls, built hundreds of years ago, still proclaiming the mighty labours of former generations. No signs of life or human habitation, an atmosphere as clear as crystal; it seemed, as the sun's glorious rays, in changing colours, lit up the scene, that the presence of the Almighty was near us, and involuntarily taking off our hats, we whispered—" Magnificent !" But the deepening gloom told us we must hasten on. We were then at the summit of the pass, 2500 feet above the sea level: nothing extraordinary as regards elevation, but as regards scenery it could hardly be surpassed; so, with lingering glances on what we were leaving, we descended on foot, leaving our litters and mules to follow. We arrived at the village of Chatow at 8 P.M., and were very tired and hungry. We put up for the night, and found a comfortable hotel and a good kitchen—at least, what seemed to us to be so. The cold was increasing, our thermometer marking 38°. If sleep is the sign of contentment and of a clear conscience, such must have been our state; as after the exertions of the day, the clear bracing air, and the novelty of the life we were leading, the mind as well as the body was utterly fatigued, and, although our bed was on bare boards, no feather bed could have been more comfortable to us.

Feeling the importance of getting all the daylight we could, we left Chatow at 6 o'clock on the

22nd. It was very cold, the thermometer standing at 32°; but what made it so observable was the penetrating wind, which seemed to find its way through the thickest clothes we could muster. I have often since, when the thermometer has been 20° lower, without wind, felt the cold less. The country we passed over was perfectly barren, and not a tree to be seen; it is in fact the commencement of the Great Desert, although not called so. Passing some old forts, all more or less dilapidated, we reached at 11 o'clock the large walled town of Wun-lie-Cheong, without exception the most interesting and finest town *we* had seen since leaving Pekin. The distance was about thirteen miles from Chatow. Just before arriving here one of our guides, who was entertaining me with a long account of something, to me, perfectly unintelligible, brought his mule close to my litter, which his animal disapproving of, shot him over his head into a pool of water, and very nearly capsized me again. Our unfortunate Tartar came out of his bath very much sobered, and after belabouring his mule, which seemed to afford him much satisfaction, got on him again as if nothing had happened. He must have been very cold, as it was blowing about as hard as it could. Before entering the town we crossed over a very beautiful old bridge with five arches, and standing by itself, about 250 feet off, was another arch, which I have no doubt, at some remote period, must have been attached to the bridge then spanning a much larger river. The town also affords evidence that its former inhabitants must have been industrious, wealthy people, as the walls are large and solid, still in good preservation, and the whole appearance of the town is better than any we have seen.

For the first time for many months we now saw ice, the ponds we passed being all more or less frozen. We reached Sha-Shing, a moderate sized walled town, where we rested for the night, having made during the day about twenty-eight miles. Somehow or other I could not sleep: the moon shining so brightly through the windows of our room, which were made of paper, and the howling of the wind, kept me awake, and without being able to account for it, a feeling of uneasiness grew upon me. Finding I could not sleep, I was in the act of rising when our door slowly opened, and a head introduced itself, cautiously looking round the room. I must say first that a sense of loneliness, so far away from all civilisation, and a feeling of how utterly isolated we were, gave me a decided feeling of fear; but my revolver, which was close to me, and upon which I knew I could rely, somehow or other found its way into my hand. I never moved, being anxious to see the result. I must explain here that every night we were in the habit of having all our baggage in our room with us, and we had of necessity a good quantity of Sycee silver to pay our way—more than we wanted, as it turned out. My fellow-traveller was fast asleep, so I waited quietly, until my Chinese friend, seeing all was quiet, stole in and made his way to the bag in which all our silver was. How he knew it was there I cannot imagine, unless our servants had told him, which is most likely. I waited until his hand was on it, when I rose, and cocking my revolver with a click, presented it at him. The effect was instantaneous: John Chinaman dropped the bag, and commenced a volley of explanations. In the meantime Mr. Walcott awoke, and seeing the Chinaman, would have shot him; but he thought better of it; so letting him go, we put all our baggage against the door. It may be well imagined that after this we could not sleep. It was useless for us to make an inquiry next morning; so we left, feeling well contented to be so lucky, as, had we lost our Sycee, we should have been in a great strait.

Two or three days in a litter takes away any further desire to travel in it any longer. No invention for giving the cramp could be more perfect. So on starting again next morning we decided to push on as fast as possible. But guides, all over the world, are very much the same; ours had all manner of difficulties ready for invention, and proved as obstinate as their own mules. We started again at 6 A.M., and after a pleasant ride of five hours, the wind having moderated, we came to Chi-Ming-Yie, where we stopped for lunch. We walked most of the day, and began to feel now that the wind had moderated, what a splendid climate we were in! Nearly all day we journeyed through a long valley surrounded on all sides by lofty mountains—on the west side by a long snow range. We could trace the course of a river far off to the west, and the only trees we could see were on its banks. We were going over sand and stones. Villages and towns are here scarce, but old forts, like Martello towers, all in ruins, line the road at about two miles apart. Leaving the valley, we followed the left bank of the Yung-Ho for six or seven miles, going over a small pass cut out of the rocks, where, remembering my former accident, I preferred trusting to my legs. We saw indications of coal-mines, but not worked at present, also copper and iron. I am convinced that valuable mines exist in these parts, but the Chinese government will not permit any researches. We passed large trains of camels, laden with produce from Russia, which had been transported across the desert. The road here had formerly been good, but is now very bad. We commenced ascending gradually, and after a steady walk reached Shün-hwa-Fŭ, about 200 feet over the sea level, where we stayed the night, having made about thirty miles.

The 24th of October was a splendid day. The wind had entirely died away, and although it was cold, the thermometer standing at 28°, after the rough weather we had been undergoing it was like paradise to us. We entered thoroughly into the novelty of the life we were leading, and could appreciate the beautiful scenery we were passing through. As we wished to reach Chang-chia-Kow early we started at 3 A.M. The moon was shining brightly, and cast a brilliancy on the surrounding country only to be seen in similar climates. Proceeding still through the long valley we had entered the day before, at half-past nine we discovered, situated down in an amphitheatre of lofty mountains, the town of Chang-chia-Kow. At first it looked like a collection of rocks, the roofs of the houses all being of a stone colour. I could not help feeling glad that our journey in litters was now at an end, as four days of that sort of travelling is quite enough, as they are not the most comfortable style of conveyance; but, considering that we could not communicate with our drivers, not being able to speak their tongue, we got on very well with them, and found them willing and honest.

Chang-chia-Kow, or more commonly called by the Mongol name of Kalgan, which means "entrance gate," is situated in latitude 42° and longitude 116°, 2400 feet above the level of the sea. It is the last town in China Proper, the distance from Pekin being 147 miles. Very little verdure of any kind is seen here, and not a single tree; it is in fact the commencement of the Great Desert of Gobi. The population consists of 17,000 inhabitants, mostly Chinese and Mongols, and about ten Russian merchants, whose business consists entirely of caring for the transportation of tea across the desert. We entered the town at eleven, and a very novel sight it seemed to us after the quiet life we had been leading during the last four days. The streets are wide, and lined with some of the best shops I have seen in China. The roofs of the houses are all made of mud, on which may be seen crops of grass, which give a very curious appearance to the town. The streets were crowded with long caravans of camels, bound to Kiachta, laden with brick tea; oxen, and carts drawn by men, laden with produce from Russia, coming the other way; Mongols, camel-drivers, hurrying here and there, mounted on ponies or camels, keeping the stragglers together, dressed in various-coloured clothes, and looking most picturesque. The sight presented to us was so different to anything we had ever seen before—it was like the realisation of one of the scenes in the 'Arabian Nights' tales. I felt thoroughly bewildered. If bustle and animation are a sign of prosperity, Kalgan must be ranked foremost in that category, and I believe it is the most prosperous town in China for its size. We were jammed in one of the streets for fully an hour, and my attention was entirely concentrated on the rocking about of my litter as we jolted against camels and carts, &c.; but at last, by taking a detour, and leaving the town by passing under a low arch, before we could get through which we had to descend from our litters, we got clear of the Babel, and passing through the suburbs noticed some first-rate Chinese houses.

E

built with more appearance of comfort than those in other parts of China. Here we found the house of a Russian merchant, to whom we had letters of introduction, and on whose firm we had letters of credit. We hardly expected to be lodged, but only wished to inquire for the best inn. We were, however, most hospitably received and our luggage at once unladen, and informed that, as long as we liked to remain in Kalgan, we were welcome to a shelter and what turned out to be every species of attention. I shall never forget the kindnesses I have experienced from Russians throughout my journey; but here it was doubly welcome, as, utterly friendless and without any knowledge of the language, we should have been in a very unpleasant strait, and we could never have succeeded in making the arrangements for crossing the desert, so well or so quickly as we did, without their aid. The Mongols believe that Mongolia is the centre of the world, bounded by China on one side and Russia on the other; and it would be perfectly useless to try and persuade them that there are other nations. They have a great respect for Russians, and it is always necessary to pass for one in order to facilitate travelling in this part of the world. It is next to useless for any Englishman who may be inclined to make this journey to go to Kalgan without introductory letters to some Russian merchant. It is no easy matter to make proper arrangements for speedily crossing the desert even then ; but to attempt to do so without Russian aid is simply a waste of days and days, and probably double the expense, and then with a most imperfect result, as, without exception, the Mongols are the most difficult race of people to make a bargain with I have ever met. Having paid the balance due to our mule drivers, and given them drink-money, which delighted them very much, we felt perfectly easy in our minds as to the future. But here an unforeseen difficulty appeared, as our hosts could speak nothing but Russian and Chinese. Luckily our Chinese servants became valuable as interpreters, and they were of great use to us. It is necessary, and I say so from experience, to engage a good servant at Tientsin, as it would be next to impossible to get on at all without their assistance on the road, especially at the inns, where it is indispensable to speak Chinese. We committed an extravagance in taking two servants, as one would have been sufficient; but still I do not regret having done so, considering the real assistance they were to us.

I never could make out whether our kind Russian hosts were under the impression that we, as a daily custom, were in the habit of eating five or six times a day, or that our appearance, which was decidedly a hungry one, denoted a necessity for constant feeding; but I can only say that, during the few days I remained there, we seemed to be constantly having breakfast or dinner or supper. Perhaps they knew better than we did what was before us in Mongolia, and wished to start us in as good a condition as possible. A room was placed at our disposal with a sort of raised dais at one end, on which we placed our mattresses. This is the general kind of sleeping-room throughout the north of China. Our luggage, which we at once commenced unpacking, we grouped around the room, so as to concentrate all we had into as small a compass as possible. After being out in the open air for so long we found the atmosphere of our room nearly intolerable; it was heated up by an immense stove, and the windows, which are double ones, hermetically sealed; so that a change of air during the winter months never penetrates through the rooms.

We were interrupted by our host, whose knowledge of English was limited to the words " Drink tea," to which invitation we cheerfully responded, not having eaten for twenty hours. Here we first made acquaintance with one of the greatest Russian institutions, the *samovar*. It is a large sort of urn ; in the centre is a tube into which hot coal or charcoal is introduced, which keeps it constantly boiling. The method of making and drinking tea is also very agreeable. In a small tea-pot a strong infusion, nearly essence of tea, is made ; a small quantity of this is poured into tumblers, and each guest adds water and sugar *ad libitum*. Whether it is that the tea in Russia is much better than we get in England, or that the method of drinking it is better than ours, I know not, I can only say that I never tasted its equal before, and never hardly for years imbibed so much as I did during my short stay at Kalgan. The Russians say that the tea which makes only a land voyage is much superior to that which passes over the sea, and I am inclined to their opinion ; also, that their method of making it for drinking is the right one. We generally carried cold tea with us, which we found much better than spirits or wine of any kind.

The Russian cookery is certainly not much adapted to our tastes, every dish being more or less made with oil; but it is a well known fact that nothing is a better preservative against cold than oil—far better than spirits. I have no doubt that had I been invited in the ordinary course of life to partake of the dishes set before us I should have declined them; but hunger and exercise, in a climate which of itself gives an appetite, are wonderful levellers, and I do not think that I ever enjoyed a meal so much as I did that identical breakfast, and had not my travelling companion stopped me I should have probably drank as much tea as the young lady in the 'Pickwick Papers.' Our breakfast being finished, we now set seriously to work so as to make our arrangements for crossing to Kiachta as soon as possible. We were afraid of delaying as it was quite late enough in the season, and every day the cold winds in Mongolia became more intense.

Certainly our first impression of the Mongols was decidedly favourable; they seemed thoroughly good-natured, honest, and simple, and we began to congratulate ourselves on the prospects of getting two good guides. The Chinese, physically, compared with the Mongols, are very inferior, especially those in the north; as regards cunning and intelligence, they beat them a long way, but in making a bargain, or rather, I would say, in coming to terms, the Mongols carry the palm over all other nations.

Squatting down on their haunches, you may argue all day, or try to convince them, without success. For two hours did our hosts—taking no end of trouble, talking Mongol to the Mongols, Russian to his partner, and Chinese to our boys, who finally interpreted the sense to us—try to arrange proper terms with two Lama priests, but without the slightest success, although they listened most attentively, simply shaking their heads at intervals as sign of refusal. They then tried another guide, thinking it was good to create opposition; but it was of no use. I began to despair of ever arranging matters, but our friends told us not to be impatient—that it always took a day or so to convince a Mongol mind. The room was now full of Mongol chiefs, Lamas, &c., all of whom had heard that we were going to cross. The difficulty seemed to be that each of these various parties owned large caravans of camels, and were not willing to divide them. We only wanted six, and those who owned twenty to one hundred naturally did not care about going with us, and leaving their other camels behind, as sooner or later they were sure to find employment for them, the demand at this season being always very great for transporting tea to Kiachta. The camels are really only in travelling condition during the winter months, at the end of which time they are turned out to graze on the grassy slopes of Western Mongolia. Their two humps, when out of condition, lie flat down on their backs, whereas they become erect when fit for travelling. This condition is always a good test of a sound camel, and, in choosing, these signs should be strictly adhered to. When travelling they require very little food and scarcely any water, which latter they never get when on a constant voyage, as it puffs them out and makes them lazy. They are possessed with the most remarkable patience and endurance, and will walk along at the rate of two miles and a half per hour, with a long swing, without apparent exertion. When a camel is to be laden, the driver pulls a string, which is tied to a stick through the nose, and making a curious sort of a cry, the animal gently kneels down, first on its fore legs, and then quietly lets its hind legs down under it. The cargo or luggage is then suspended on a sort of wooden saddle covered with skins (great care being taken to avoid chafing the humps, which quickly renders them useless), in equal weights on each side, which is sufficient to keep it in its place, each camel carrying about four hundredweight. To make them rise, the driver again touches the nose-string, and with a wail like a child the huge ungainly animal rises abruptly, first on its hind legs. When mounting for riding it is necessary to know this, as without it the would-be rider finds himself flying over the camel's head. The motion of riding I have often heard compared to being at sea, and as being equally provocative of nausea. I never found it so, it seemed remarkably easy and comfortable. A caravan proceeds in a long line, each camel's nose-string being loosely tied to the hind part of the saddle of the preceding one; the string is never made firm for fear of breaking the nose, which renders them nearly useless, there being no other part of the body where a leading-string could be attached; but they only require the slightest tension of the string to keep them on their monotonous motion, which however stops the moment it becomes lax.

The camel certainly is a wonderful animal; it will work steadily across the desert eighteen hours a day, for thirty days, with scarcely any water, and with the little fodder which the desert affords.

They are entirely adapted for this part of the world, being only of service on flat plains, as on rising ground they are nearly useless. It is certainly a proof to any real thinker of the wonderful fitness of all things in this world. It is the very animal adapted to the place and is useless elsewhere, and requires little or no care, sustenance, or shelter.

We now tried a third party of Lamas, who seemed more inclined to come to terms, but still without success. I was not sorry at this moment to hear that dinner was ready, it now being three o'clock, as I was becoming rapidly confused by the various languages spoken, and could hardly gather the purport of the parley as interpreted to me. The shades of evening were falling, and the lofty mountain situated in front of the house, over whose crests we could trace parts of the celebrated great Wall of China, with its towers and gates, stood out in bold relief. It was wonderful how fine the outlines of the hills were rendered by the excessive clearness of the atmosphere. The cold warned me (I was then standing in the verandah) that I had better retire into the house. It also began to make me feel doubtful as to my outfit for crossing the desert. It was very strange indeed to us to feel cold after the fearful heat we had been enduring in the south, but, I must say, a very pleasant sensation.

Washing is a custom observed in this part of the world, but only under peculiar circumstances. Finding no implements necessary for ablutions in our room we shouted for the servant, and by dint of signs, rubbing our hands together as if washing, &c., at last made his very slow brain comprehend us. Beckoning us into the hall, he introduced us to a queer sort of a machine, which proved to be the family washing apparatus. He left us there to our reflections. Looking all round it, I failed to discover any method of getting water out of it. It was a sort of brass barrel attached to the wall, and, underneath, a huge copper basin. Taking off the cover, I could see water inside, but how to get at it still remained a mystery. Suddenly I discovered a sort of button underneath, which looked like an ornament; without the remotest idea that this was the tap, I pressed it, and out came a volume of water right down my sleeve, which was more than I wanted. However, by holding my finger upwards, and pressing the button, my friend holding the basin, we had nearly filled it, when we were interrupted by a laugh from our Russian host, who was standing behind us. He then taught us the method of using this quaint machine. You press the button with the hand gently; some six or eight drops of water fall into the hand, which you transfer to the face. This being done, a family towel, which, however, is not very necessary for the amount of water, hangs conveniently beside you. A sort of a rub on the hands completes the effort; in fact, what is generally called a dry wash. However, as we got accustomed to this apparatus we squandered the water fearfully—so evidently thought our Chinese domestic.

Finding we still could not arrange for camels we proceeded in the moonlight to the yard of a cart contractor, and without much difficulty picked up two old conveyances, which we were to have the use of to Kiachta, paying here for them the very moderate sum of fifteen taels each, or £4 10s. We found out, afterwards, that it is better to hire than buy a cart, as it saves all trouble of disposing of it at Kiachta; but I must say from experience that were I ever to cross the desert again, which may the Fates forbid! I should go to the expense of having a first-rate cart built. It should be fully six feet long. Mine, which looked like an old bathing machine on two wheels without springs, was only five feet six inches long and three broad, so that I could never once stretch myself out at full length—a state of affairs which at times became unbearable. It is necessary to have a good cart, as, journeying all night, it makes a tolerably decent sleeping conveyance. It should be made as light as possible, to open at the side, as the wind blowing from the front comes through any opening there, and windows, provided with shutters, in case the glass breaks, which it invariably does; plenty of hooks, a shelf, and I should advise it to be four feet broad. Our carts were to be entirely put in order, relined with felt, and all cracks, &c., made good by the next day at 5 P.M.

When we returned we found two Lama priests, who had been quietly digesting our offers, ready to make the following terms, but not until we had gone through another hour's wrangle. It was arranged that we were to start on the 28th. They were to give us six camels, and make good if any should break down on the way. If we arrived in Kiachta in twenty-three days, we were to pay them 100 taels, including everything; in twenty-two days, 104 taels; in twenty-one days, 110; and in twenty, 114; but for this we said we would give 120, so as to spur them on; if twenty-four days, only 96 taels; and each day longer, 4 taels less. We were to pay down 100 taels, and receive an agreement from them, written in Russian and Chinese, stamped by the Chinese authorities; and it was agreed, if over time on arrival at Kiachta, that we should sell one of their camels, and deduct from the price it realised the amount of forfeiture.

A load fell off my mind, as I had anticipated that days would be lost before we could have arrived at so satisfactory an arrangement. Without our Russian friends we should never have succeeded. The trouble they took was very great, and, although I could only express my sincere gratitude to them in English, I am sure they understood the sense, if not the exact meaning, of my words.

It was amusing how we got on with our Russian friends by signs, and before we left them we had established a code of signals comprehensible to both sides. It was extremely ludicrous at times, but it afforded us much enjoyment and food for laughter. Having partaken of our fifth meal at eight o'clock, when we were obliged to eat of everything for fear of offending our host, I retired to our room, and, to my great disgust, found the large stove blazing away with an enormous fire, and, as we could not open the windows, we were half stifled. However, the sense of having done a good day's work and a feeling of ease as to the future lulled me to sleep. Rising early next morning we first of all arranged our baggage, so as to have all handy in our carts, dividing the stores between us in case it should become too cold to picnic together in the wilderness. We then ordered each a large goat-skin cover, two pairs of felt socks, and a fur cap, such as are worn by the Mongols themselves (it covers the head and face, except the eyes). A list of stores, &c., which our kind hosts prepared for us, may prove useful to future travellers by this route : A teapot, a large saucepan, one cup, one large bowl, candles and a Chinese lantern, a hatchet, and plenty of rope ; bread, meat, vegetables, sugar, and a few bottles of wine and spirits, which we found, to our sorrow, fell short on the way; plenty of biscuits, good thick sheepskin coats, and plenty of pillows, completed our outfit.

All our wants now being supplied, we took a walk round to the yard to see after our carts, and found carpenters busily engaged refitting and making them strong ; so we had only to make a few suggestions as to comfort. After the usual lunch and tumblers of tea, we inquired for ponies, as, having our saddles with us, we thought it would much relieve the monotony of our journey. Two very good ones were soon shown us, and as we intended paying a visit to Mr. Yulick, an American missionary who resides in the city, we signified our intention of riding them there on trial. But this was easier to imagine than to accomplish, as Tartar ponies, first of all, are not accustomed to our saddles and bridles, and secondly, object decidedly to do any thing against their own will. A short trial of who was the strongest, enforced by a good whip, soon brought them to terms, and we proceeded quietly to the city. We found the road very rough and dirty, and we had much difficulty in getting past the long strings of camels and ox carts, but at last we arrived safely at our destination. Mr. Yulick was very pleased to see us, as it is not often that foreigners have been so far. He kindly wrote us down a list of words and phrases, which turned out to be of great service to us in the desert. Returning again, and squeezing through the streets, we found the owners of the ponies waiting; but as they asked fifty taels for each, which was much too dear, we decided to wait, as we were told that in the desert we could buy good ponies for ten taels, which proved to be the case. The spluttering *samovar* again absorbed our attention. The day being still young, and just the weather for walking, we ascended the hill in front of our house and visited the Great Wall, the height we reached being about 4000 feet over the sea level. The wall itself we found in ruins, but still it gives a good idea of what it must have been. Its extent, according to the Chinese, is upwards of 3000 miles; probably however this is an exaggeration. In some parts it runs along the tops of high ridges and mountain peaks. How the bricks and stones were carried up is a wonder. I must say, having heard so much of this wall, I was very much disappointed with it, I scarcely know why. I do not think, except to say that one has been close to it, that it repays even a climb up the hills to see it. This I am afraid is considered a species of heresy by those who have never visited it, but by those who have I do not doubt my opinion is approved. But the scenery, taking the wall itself out of the question, is superb, and that certainly does repay the traveller all the discomfort he may have gone through in order to arrive at this spot.

F

This was to be our last evening, and I could not help feeling a sensation of extreme loneliness stealing over me when I reflected how long a time we should probably be without seeing any traces of civilisation, and through what an unknown country we were going to pass twenty-three days, and amongst a nearly unknown race of people. However, it was now too late to think of receding—not that for one moment did such a desire come over me. A mutual attachment had sprung up between our kind friends and ourselves, and we may be forgiven if we bid a rather sorrowful good-night to them.

I could hardly sleep during this night, so rose early in the morning of the 26th and took a short stroll before breakfast. The thermometer showed ten degrees of frost, and the bracing pure air soon drove away any dismal thoughts I had been indulging in. It is curious, when we are so far away from home, especially in a barbarous country, and not knowing how and when, or indeed if ever, we shall see it again, how intensely we long to be there, and how greatly magnified seem to be the difficulties of the route. And when it is all over and forgotten how anxious we feel to be off again!

At 10 A.M. our camels appeared, and we were pleased with their appearance. Our whole baggage only weighed four hundredweight, which we divided between two camels, being only half of the quantity they were accustomed to carry. We then sped them on their journey, we intending to follow four hours later in our carts, which were to be drawn over the steep pass of Kalgan by ponies, as camels are of no use for this purpose. The latter animals, it was arranged, should wait for us at the commencement of the desert. Having partaken of a final meal —which, with a presentiment of short commons for many days, we made a good one—we wished our kind hosts, through the medium of our servants, adieu. We had passed a very happy time with them. I do not believe that under any circumstances could we have received more genuine kindness than we did, and it was difficult for me to express my sense of it; a lump would rise in my throat, which I could not prevent. After kissing all the men, on the lips—I would much have preferred kissing the ladies—we passed through the door, when our Russian host solemnly devoted us to the care of the Almighty, and wished us every happiness. They then all accompanied us about a mile on our way, and finally bade adieu. We walked steadily ahead without speaking for some time, the state of our feelings not allowing us to break silence. We were followed by our carts. But as the grandeur of the scene broke upon us, and the glories of the atmosphere shone round us, we cheered up, and, throwing all sense of loneliness away, we soon began to speak cheerily and make speculations as to the journey before us. The road was tremendously rough, full of rocks and stones. Before starting I had arranged my cart in a most scientific manner, hanging up all I should require on nails, and arranging my pillows and wraps as comfortably as possible. Jolt, jolt, came the springless cart over the stones, and never for a moment did I imagine the awful effect it was producing on my arrangements, over which I had spent so much trouble; but feeling tired, we thought to try our carts. I heard an exclamation of horror from my friend as he climbed into his machine, and another burst from me as I got into mine; for every single thing lay in the centre of the cart—pillows, rugs, brushes, all jumbled up together; candles flying about, and a bottle of sherry broken into small atoms. One of the windows was also broken: an incalculable disaster, as I had no means of repairing it, but had always in future to stuff a pillow in, or I should have been frozen. As fast as I endeavoured to put things in order again they were bumped out of their places; so I resigned myself to my fate, and tried to rest comfortably in the midst of this confusion. But I could not stand it very long, being thrown about in all directions, and having my head nearly broken by a large bag, which still remained suspended, falling upon it. With a great deal of effort I extricated myself from the cart, preferring to walk all night rather than endure such torment any more. I found my companion had also descended from his cart, so we walked along at a good pace, the increasing cold—all the ponds we passed being frozen—keeping us from loitering.

We reached the summit of this truly magnificent pass at 6 P.M., and although it is only 6500 feet above the sea level, for scenery it stands alone in its glory. I have been over many passes in my life, but never have I seen such a sight as burst upon us when, reaching the summit, we halted to gain breath. As far as the eye could reach, ranges of hills and snow-clad mountains, like confused waves tossing on the ocean, rose before us.

We could trace the Great Wall, extending its span over the mountain tops, and could see the various towers standing solitary in their ruins. A valley lay at our feet, through which, like a silver line, a small river was wending its way, and the path we had been toiling up for four hours we could distinctly discern. The scene, in wildness, surpassed anything that the most fertile imagination could dream of, so utterly rugged and variegated was it. We stood in its midst, the only evidence of life; and deeply feeling the grandeur of all we saw, and remembering that all these wonders were made for man, we were overpowered.

The sun was now setting, and it would be impossible for me to describe the magnificence of the now changing panorama before us. The perfect clearness of the atmosphere, the deep purple on the hills, and the ever-changing colours cast by the declining sun on the mountains around us, were perfectly bewildering, and we could only hold our breath and wonder. If such a picture could be painted, few people would believe that it was a faithful transcript of nature. I only wish that I could write all that I felt then, and give but a slight account of the scene. But my pen fails me, and could never do even the slightest justice to the scene. I can only say that from this moment I felt that to witness this sight repaid us for going through double the discomforts and exertions that we had passed through. Tearing ourselves away, as the darkness now rapidly descended over the scene, we passed through the Great Wall and found ourselves in Mongolia. Leaving China behind us, we entered our carts again; as we were descending the ponies proceeded at a trot. I forbear to mention the agonies we suffered, until we arrived, at twelve o'clock, on the sandy plains of the desert, having made thirty miles. We here found our camels and guides waiting for us; a tent pitched, a comfortable fire, and some hot water simmering in a huge sort of kettle, which, with a little whisky, somewhat cheered our bruised bodies. As we were to start at 2 A.M. I retired into my cart in order to get a little sleep, having somewhat arranged it, intending to make it more comfortable when daylight should appear.

Before finally bidding adieu to China, as we passed through the Great Wall, I suspend my narrative for a short space, and with the reader's permission, ere I enter Mongolia, would make a few brief remarks regarding our present relations with China, and recent events which have occurred in connection with them. When the last treaty was ratified, in October 24, 1860, called the 'British Treaty,' certain conditions were stipulated upon. Other nations, to a great extent, came in also under this treaty, and so it has been the case that Chinese officials have learned to look upon England as the representative foreign power in China. Now, when England withdraws her fleet, neglects to protect her subjects, snubs her consuls for doing their duty, —*vide* Mr. Gibson, who, for doing his strict duty was snubbed and disgraced, and died of a broken heart. But what of that? Peace to his remains! To save the nation perhaps a few thousand pounds, a fleet, which is necessary, is gradually allowed to die out; and when war comes, as come it will, an outlay will have to be incurred costing a million, just through this little penny-wise proceeding. Other nations ask, Why did England take precedence if she had no intention of keeping up the treaty? When Chinese mandarins see signs of weakness in England all nationalities suffer alike, as they discern no difference in the foreigner. It is to be presumed that the trade with China is worth keeping up. Tea and silk are very necessary commodities to England. The export trade from Manchester and other manufacturing towns is large and increasing. It is downright short-sighted policy we are pursuing with the Chinese, and it will be found out when new complications arise and other powers take the lead out of our hands. I believe many old residents in China look upon a row as certain in a year or two. Many of the most intelligent and most respectable among the Chinese merchants do, and deplore it much.

I would never advocate force of arms, but would make the Chinese officials see that we are determined to make them stick to the treaty. A war with China would be a far different affair to the old one. They are now well armed, their forts are rebuilt, and they have learned much in discipline and military art from us and other powers.

That any statesman could have received the Burlinghame mission is, and will always remain, a marvel to those who know China well. The mandarins hardly expected it, and must have laughed considerably in their sleeves at the result. The treaty is " addressed from the Emperor of China, the whole world, sun, moon, &c., to the tributary powers of the west." The Chinese who accompanied Mr. Burlinghame were not first-rate. It would be a curious embassy if a Chinaman were sent to Pekin to represent England, and, of course, it would not be accepted; but not a bit more than that an American should be sent from Pekin to negotiate a treaty for China with foreign powers. It is simply an insult, and a mere ruse, to enable the Chinese authorities, when it suits their convenience, to ignore a treaty so negotiated, saying, with perfect truth, that it was arranged by a foreigner. It states also that the Chinese are daily advancing in civilisation, that they are amicably inclined, and well disposed towards foreigners. This is so far untrue as the writer, on various occasions, only a few miles in the interior, has been very roughly treated: a clear proof of the good disposition of the Chinese towards foreigners. The mission is a sham and a blind, and this time will show. The age has passed for a community of intelligent merchants who reside in China to be classed as pirates and smugglers. Although they are still designated as "irate traders," some deference should be paid to their opinions. People on the spot generally know more about the country than those who have never been there; and those people, with few exceptions, condemn entirely England's present policy, and the acceptance of the Burlinghame mission. I hope, in making this brief digression, I have not exceeded my reader's patience; but I cannot help looking upon this subject, so full of important interest, as not understood in England. Can it be doubted that it is a question of serious import, whether we shall continue to hold our own in China, or allow other nations to gradually absorb the trade which it has taken so much trouble and expense to create?

There are only a few more subjects that I would allude to before closing this chapter, and one of them is the maintenance of an English church at the open ports.

At nearly every open port an English church exists, which government had formerly afforded a small support to, amounting in all to some three or four thousand pounds per annum. It does incalculable good, not only by example, but as a proof of England's reverence for religion, and excites admiration amongst all classes and sects of the communities who attend its services on the Sabbath. At some of the ports, where the residents are few, it has, even with this aid, been found very difficult to keep up the building and maintain the chaplain. But to save a few pounds, which would be spent in a few trips of a new gunboat, the government has withdrawn this small grant, and so virtually closed the only buildings where, at each port, residents of all classes were accustomed to meet every Sunday and worship the Almighty. I have heard dissenters from the Church of England regret this, as, although differing from her doctrines, they look upon the existence of a church at each port as a proof to the Chinese mind of the fact of Christianity.

Another and last remark is, with reference to the reduction being made in consuls' salaries, which have never been large enough. The representative of England should have enough to live on and keep up a little dignity. With his present salary this is in all instances, with the exception of Pekin, where the minister is overpaid for doing nothing, impossible. Living in China is very expensive, and the climate is not such a one as to induce intelligent men, which consuls should be, and are, as a rule, to spend years of their lives in it without being able to save a penny, nay, barely to exist on their income. How can they represent British interests justly? I cannot help thinking that people, if they only knew these facts, would feel ashamed that such a wretched mean policy should be pursued by a nation like England. One could hardly understand even Germany so disgracing herself.

CHAPTER III.

The Start—In our Carts, harnessed to Camels—We shoot some Hawks, to the Astonishment of the Guides, who have never seen a repeating Rifle fired—Our first Encampment—The Desert becomes bare of Pasture—We meet the first Caravan from Kiachta—Purchase two Ponies of a Mongol Horse-dealer—The Steed turns restive—A Tussle in the Desert—Visit from an old Mongol—Hospitality of these People—Their Habits and Occupations—Sunrise in the Desert—Our Camels break down—A Mongol Venus—A Visit to one of the *Yourts*, or Tents — Bargaining for fresh Camels—Want of Water—A Mirage in the Desert—Intruders join us—Knocked up at night in my Cart by one of them asking for Liquor—Fire my Revolver in reply—My new Camel turns restive, and nearly pitches me out of my Cart—The Plain covered with Camel's Bones—The horrible Cold of a North-easter—The effect of the Atmosphere in magnifying distant Objects—Attempt to steal our Camels by mounted Mongols—We name our Mongol Lama Guides 'Monkey' and 'Cocoanut'—The Cold increasing—Our Ponies getting starved for want of Fodder—More than half frozen in my Cart: the Pain of being thawed—We reach Tsagan Tugurik—Vast Herds of Camels—We present a Mongol with some Cayenne Pepper to stop begging for Whisky — Signs of Ironstone and Copper Ore.

AFTER remaining a short time, two of our camels were harnessed in our carts, and with a splendid moon shining we proceeded slowly over the desert. I found that sleep was out of the question, as indeed we found it generally was throughout the whole journey across when we were in motion, the long swing of the camel jerking the springless carts most unmercifully. However I managed to remain in mine until 6 A.M. the next day, the 28th, when we found ourselves in the midst of a plain, not a hill being in sight, except the pass we had come over, already fading away. The altitude was 3400 feet above the sea's level, and the temperature 24° Fahrenheit. Beyond the novelty of our situation and a cold north-east wind springing up in the afternoon, little worth calling incident happened during the day. We had some long shots at large hawks with a thirteen-repeating Henry rifle, and managed to bag two fine specimens, much to the astonishment as well as somewhat to the dismay of our Lamas, who, not seeing any loading going on and never having seen a similar gun, the rapid shots seemed to them akin to magic.

At 4 P.M., having walked most of the day, we encamped, intending to remain until 10 P.M., so as to give the camels a short halt, which they require every eighteen hours, and to get some food for ourselves, having eaten nothing since leaving Kalgan; our guides also requiring a short sleep, which they took in turns, one always keeping watch. As soon as the halt was called the camels were all made to kneel down, unladen, and taken out of their carts; they were then allowed to pick up any fodder they could find for about an hour, but were seldom given any water, as it makes them lazy; they were then all collected together and made to kneel down, where they remained chewing the cud until the start was made again. As soon as we halted, our first care, whilst our Lamas were pitching a common tent, made of a sort of blue canvas, was to get our carts in order; we then overhauled our stores and cooked our dinner—mutton broth and biscuits—which we had every day when water was obtainable as long as we were in the desert, and, as the reader may suppose, it became rather monotonous. We had to be sparing with our stores, as we did not know when we might be able to replenish them.

In order to make a fire, in the centre of the tent we placed a sort of iron circle on legs, inside of which—there being no wood or coals obtainable—*argolots* are placed. They are composed of dry cow-dung, and at times we had difficulty in obtaining it; but whenever we came across a *yourt* we purchased for a small quantity of brick tea, as much as our sacks, which we carried for the purpose, would hold. It lights very easily, and gives a good heat, but the smoke from it is blinding, especially as there is no outlet for it at the top of the tent; but we soon discovered that by keeping in a recumbent position we avoided a good deal of it, as, on rising, it finds a gradual outlet through the door. On the morning of the 29th we found ourselves gradually leaving all signs of pasture; grass was scarce, and the only fodder a sort of a stunted heath. About the middle of the day we came across a caravan, composed of about fifty camels, laden with produce from Kiachta, and large droves of Tartar ponies. The guides, who were fine stalwart-looking fellows, surrounded us, and looked with astonishment on us, especially when they heard that we were on our way to Kiachta, which even they considered a matter of some difficulty and hardship at this season of the year. They were most amiable, simple people, and were much delighted by a revolver and a large knife I showed them, and many were their exclamations of wonder. Being anxious to purchase one pony, which we considered would be enough for both of us to get a ride for an hour or two each day, we picked a fine little animal out of a large drove and inquired the price, which was named at twenty taels, about £6; not dear for a handsome fiery little steed. But thinking we could do better perhaps later on, as our guides had, whenever we made signs to them about purchasing ponies, explained that there were plenty further on which we could get cheap, we offered ten taels. This we did by making with a stick ten strokes in the sand, to which the Mongol horse-dealer added six more; but after the usual waste of time in concluding a bargain we got him for eleven taels, and proceeded on our way rejoicing. But we had rather calculated without our host. Our caravan had proceeded onwards with one of the Lamas, the other remaining with us, so I took hold of the halter of our newly-acquired purchase, and led him on. Not being followed immediately by the Lama with us, who remained behind to receive a portion of what we had paid, for his trouble in getting a purchaser, it was no easy matter to persuade the Tartar pony to advance, probably never having seen a stranger like myself, and being unwilling to leave the drove and knowing the horrors of the desert ahead. We should have either had to remain an indefinite period in the desert or I should have been forced to relinquish my hold, for he refused to advance a step forward, and every time my travelling companion attempted to approach him from behind he lashed out and nearly pulled me over. All this time our caravan in advance was gradually getting smaller on the horizon. However, our second Lama coming up relieved us of the halter, and cantered forward on his camel, leading the now more willing steed, and we had a good hard walk before we reached our caravan again. Nothing is so tiring as endeavouring to reach anything which is continually advancing, however slow the pace.

Being anxious to try our new purchase, when we came up with the caravan we got one of the saddles from our baggage and attempted to place it on the pony's back. But this was easier said than done, and our Lamas were of no use, not understanding such saddles as we had. Theirs are generally made of wood, which sit on the animals' backs like small chairs, and the stirrups are huge affairs.

It was rather dangerous work, but at last, after some trouble, we managed to throw the saddle across and get it buckled on. My friend Mr. Walcott mounted him, and a precious hard job he had to keep his seat. Before we halted we met another drove of ponies, and I picked out one that seemed the most quiet of the lot. The price asked was twenty taels, but after a good deal of bargaining and correct weighing of the lumps of silver, I got possession for ten taels, and was very well satisfied with my purchase. The two animals were an extra trouble for the Lamas to lead, so they were attached to the rear camel, when they speedily pulled the baggage-saddle off that animal, and nearly pulled his nose out besides.

The scenery was becoming very monotonous. All the ponds of water we passed were hard frozen, and here and there large patches of snow appeared. We encamped at half-past four, very hungry and tired, no signs of habitation near us, and very little pasture, which our camels and ponies soon made the most of. The weather had become dull and heavy clouds were hanging over us, and a strong north-east wind blowing; altogether a rather gloomy aspect, especially as signs of rain appeared, which, in our unprotected state, would have been misery to us, as it would easily find its way through our carts. But "sufficient for the day is the evil thereof" proved a true adage, for our usual soup soon dispelled all feelings of gloom.

An old Mongol paid us a visit, and, squatting down on his haunches in our tent, shared our dinner, much to his satisfaction. We always regretted our inability to converse with the natives, as, no doubt, we should have derived much curious knowledge. It never seemed to trouble them whether we could understand or not, as they kept up a continual chatter, we nodding or saying " *Sign*," which means " good," in reply. The rules of hospitality are strictly observed amongst the Mongols; and however wearisome it was to us at times to have our tent, when we were eating, crowded with unasked children of the desert, we took care never to show our feelings, as it would have injured us much in their estimation. Some people laugh at such notions as respecting the prejudices of the people they are travelling amongst, and make, with very bad taste, determined efforts to offend them, and are then astonished that they sometimes come to grief. I always found that by simply endeavouring as well as I could to do as these natives did when I was in their company, and to avoid all scoffing or sneering at their religious as well as domestic arrangements, I got on well with them; and besides, I discovered a great deal that was good and even noble existed amongst them. Whenever we came across a yourt, riding up to it, we received a hearty welcome, were seated in the best place, supplied with milk, for which we generally gave some little coin, more as a curiosity, and not as payment; and from what I saw I am persuaded they would share with a stranger anything they had at the time. Free from avarice, and other vices but little known amongst them, I cannot help heartily wishing that civilisation, falsely so called, with its bottle of schnaps, will not encroach among these honest children of the desert for many a year yet to come. Their habit of life is simple and abstemious. Born in the desert, trained when quite young to ride on horseback, they are the finest although the most ugly riders in the world. They may be said to live on horseback. They used to come swooping down at full gallop right up to us, jump off their horses, quickly tie their two forelegs together, and were down on their haunches by our side in a moment. Having satisfied their curiosity they were up and off again as quick as lightning. They are long-lived. I have seen many over eighty and ninety, and looking still strong and hale. Their great occupation is tending their flocks of sheep and cows and large droves of ponies. They wander about to all parts of the desert, according to the seasons, in search of grazing ground, so that where a village of yourts may be found to day no trace may remain of it on the morrow.

Rising early from my cart on the 30th, to our great joy we found that all symptoms of rain had disappeared and not a cloud was to be seen. Those who have not seen a sunrise in the desert cannot imagine how wonderful it is, and what a purity there is in the clear crystal air canopied by a sky of dazzling blue. We calculated we were now ninety miles from the commencement of the desert, and here it becomes very sandy and uninteresting, with hardly any signs of pasture to be seen.

Passing early by a few yourts, one of our Lamas rode forward on our pony and got us some milk in two bottles we carried with us. This we found, whenever we could get it, most welcome to us. The thermometer to-day was 38°, with a strong south-westerly wind blowing, otherwise it would have been warm. We encamped again at half-past four, having done a good day's work, about thirty-six miles, since ten last evening. There was little or no fodder for the camels; they, however, did not seem to care about it; but the ponies looked very disconsolate, but ate all they could find. To day we cooked a capital dinner—beef, soup with carrots, biscuits, and mutton, chops and kidneys to follow, which, with a little cheese, a glass of sherry, and a small tin mug of old potheen to follow, made a feed for a hungry man that a king might envy. The wind was abating, and it was a beautiful clear night, the thermometer standing at 28°. I could not sleep at all, the road, as was usually the case at night, appearing very rough, and I got so jolted about that I could hardly remain in the cart. I rose again at 7 A.M., and it was a splendid morning, without a cloud to be seen; thermometer 16°. My sponge and everything in cart frozen, in which state they remained until we reached Kiachta. The wind had entirely gone down. We passed during the day large flocks of very fine sand-grouse. They flew close to us, and I very much regretted that in leaving Shanghae I had forgotten to take my fowling-piece, as I could have shot plenty easily, and they are very good eating.

Two of our camels were showing symptoms of breaking down, so one of our Lamas rode ahead in search of two others. A new Mongol joined us to-day, and we understood he was to go with us to Kiachta. He was not a Lama. He turned out to be an honest willing lad, and as long as he remained with us proved very useful. At one o'clock our Lama joined us with some new camels, attended by a whole tribe of Mongols, the father of the family, mother, sons, and daughters—all on ponies. The women dress exactly like men, and also ride in the same manner, so that it is most difficult to discover the sexes. The women are generally good-looking, strongly made, and appear very healthy. They have not the peculiar cast in the eyes which the Chinese women have, but perfectly bright black ones, and rather high cheek bones. They are excessively fond of finery, and wear quantities of glass beads in their hair and on their dress, which made me at times regret that I had none with me to give away. Whenever I gave them a small Hong Kong ten cent piece they were delighted, and made signs that they would use them as ear-rings. For a few beads we could have got anything they had. I remember one morning riding up to a yourt to ask for milk, and a very handsome dark Mongol woman came out and invited us in. Her husband soon joined her, and I never experienced in civilised society more genuine kindness and hospitality than I did from them. They seemed delighted to see us, cooked some of our chocolate and milk together, which we shared with them, and they expressed great pleasure at the sweet taste of the chocolate. When I rose to leave I gave the woman two small coins, at which she testified the greatest delight, holding them up to her ears and then showing them to her husband. As she stood up her magnificent black hair, loosely done up, fell down, and it nearly reached the ground. She was a tall woman with a dark flashing eye and well-formed shape, and as she stood a painter would have been in raptures with her and a poet would have exalted her into a heroine. When we left they both came out, the husband holding my pony as I mounted; often, as we looked behind, we saw them still standing at their door looking after us. It is quite refreshing, after the falseness and absurdities of what is called polite society, to find oneself thrown amongst a barbarian people. I believe in true manners and real innocence and kindness the latter are immeasurably superior to the former. I have no doubt these two, being all alone in the midst of the desert, often afterwards thought of our visit, and wondered who the strangers could have been who could not talk to them except with signs. I know that I benefited much by my intercourse with the Mongols. They opened my mind to the fact, that after all our system is very imperfect. I would not for a moment say in all cases that civilisation is not better than what is often falsely called barbarism, but I most unhesitatingly do aver that these people are better as they are, and would shame, even by their rude breeding, many polite people who consider themselves highly bred.

I do not think I have described the appearance of a yourt. They vary in size, being however generally about ten to twelve feet in diameter. They are made perfectly round, of thick felt, double or treble, and are quite waterproof. About two feet from the ground inside is a sort of trellis work of bamboo, which is placed and fixed some depth in the ground, and gives great strength, which is necessary against the strong winds. A ventilator is fixed at the top, which can be opened and shut at pleasure, in order to allow the smoke of the ever-burning fire, which is in the centre of the yourt, to escape. All round are strewn skins to lie down upon, their method of repose being either recumbent or on their haunches. Old bows and arrows, flint guns, and all the valuables, hang round or are placed on shelves. These yourts have only one room. They are easily struck and pitched again wherever the owner decides on remaining. Robbery being hardly known, the door is a simple flap of thick felt, which hangs from the top of a frame of bamboo, and on entering with the usual greeting, "*Mendo sign*," this has to be pushed on one side. Some of the yourts, belonging to chiefs of clans, are very luxurious compared to others. They all look clean and afford good shelter in the winter months. It is generally a sign when a few yourts are found together that water is near, and probably pasture also.

Now commenced a serious affair: our Lamas picking out two new camels in exchange for our tired ones. Of course this entailed the usual amount of bargaining, which ended, much to our annoyance, in our encamping at two o'clock. For two long hours did our Lamas wrangle, and then at last a bargain was made. Camels are not worth much here, as the small amount of silver handed over to the Mongol family (about ten shillings worth and a little brick tea, with the old camels to boot) testified. Mongols have a peculiar mode of striking a bargain. It is first necessary that the whole party interested sit down in a circle on their haunches; then, after a grave silence, commences a perfect Babel, every one speaking at the same time; the bargain at last concluded, the seller places his hand up the sleeve of the buyer. This is a contract; it is then clenched with a drink of tea, or sometimes, when available, a small glass of spirits. We found that our Lamas had a bottle with them, which they used to produce whenever a bargain was very tough. They never seemed however to drink any themselves, it being unlawful for a priest to drink wine or spirits.

The new camels had to be tried in our carts, to which they evinced great repugnance, but after taking them backwards and forwards a few times they settled down quietly to their fate. We calculated now that all our camels, with the exception of the two new ones, had been three days without food or water, and we had seen nothing but sand during that time, and all the water that we could get was by melting snow, which generally was very dirty, but we were too glad to get any to be particular. We had seen a well to-day, but found the water dirty and brackish; even our ponies, which were very hard up for water, would not drink it. During the day we saw some very beautiful mirages. One of them was very plain. On one side of us seemed to be a large blue lake surrounded by mountains covered with trees. On its banks were small hills surmounted by ruined castles. At the same time, right in front, we could discern what seemed the sea, calm as glass, with islands on it. As we advanced these pictures receded, and towards dusk faded away entirely. I was very glad to see even these delusions, as the continual monotony of the desert was becoming most wearisome.

Our course was north-west by north, and every day it was becoming colder. Hitherto we had escaped the strongest east winds, but our Lamas used to make us feel very uncomfortable by their predictions; as we had heard, and later experience convinced us of the fact, that a north-east wind in the Desert of Gobi is about the height of human misery and as much as human nature can stand. Every day when we encamped, from 4 P.M. until 10 P.M., we used to say to our Mongol guides, "Hor-dan yabo Kiachta, lang mongo joss," which means, "Go quickly to Kiachta, and you shall have plenty of money;" and then, holding up their fingers, they would signify how many days they thought it would take. We had now been but four days in the desert; it seemed like four weeks; and when twenty fingers were held up as the remaining number of days before us, we could not help feeling that it was interminably long. But after all, I cannot help looking backward to that part of our journey with pleasure. It was perfect freedom, and we were certainly gaining perfect health.

During the night we were joined by two Mongols, whose appearance we did not like at all, and we were not overpleased when we heard that they were going to join our caravan; but beyond expressing our dissatisfaction in signs we could say nothing, for want of knowledge of the language. Moreover, we did not wish to create offence, as we were perfectly alone in the desert, and we could have been very easily murdered, and, of course, never heard of again. However, we arranged a signal in case anything happened, our carts being close together. I found, as the sequel proves, that the best way to discourage hangers-on to our caravan was, instead of giving the remnants of our soup to our two Lamas, which we always did, to divide it equally amongst them all; which plan, acting against the interests of the former, they themselves soon got rid of the intruders. I noticed one of these new Mongols prowling about where my cart was, so I entered it earlier than I usually did, and put my revolver in a convenient place, keeping my lamp alight. A short time before the camels were harnessed in for our usual start again at 10 P.M., my door, which was hooked inside, was violently tugged at. I jumped up and opened it, when the face of one of the Mongols appeared, and made a sign, asking me for something to drink. I suppose one of our Lamas had told them we had whisky with us. Besides being very cold, I was just getting to sleep, and I knew I should get none now all night. I did feel intensely angry. I seized my revolver, and pointed it at him for reply. Away he scudded, and I fired in the air as a warning to him. It had its effect, for during his short stay with us he never came near me. Of course my companion quickly came out of his cart, and I related to him all that happened; so we called our Lamas and expostulated with them, which produced the usual negative result, as they did not understand a word we said. I was not very sorry when we moved on again, as we were near large caravans, and the Mongols with them are very different from those who dwell in the desert. They travel about between China and Kiachta, and look more like some of the worst Chinese. I often wondered they let us by without hindrance. We took good care to show them nothing of value; whilst to the inhabitants of the yourts we showed all we had, feeling a perfect trust in them.

The whole of the 1st of November we passed over an interminable sandy plain, in which no fodder or water was to be found, and we began to fear for our poor ponies. When we first had them they were full of spirit; in fact, we could never go near them without their kicking out, but now hunger and fatigue had made them very quiet. I felt very sorry for them. I was endeavouring at noon, as I had not slept the preceding night, to get a nap in my cart, but my camel was not agreeable to the arrangement, for without any warning he suddenly sat down, and sent me nearly through the front of the cart, one of my legs going through the only remaining window I had; so now all three were broken; a nice prospect for a northeaster! Evidently my camel had made up his mind to remain as long as he could where he was, for it took a good hour and a half before we got him up again, and as soon as we got him once more into the cart he quietly sat down again; so we had to transfer our baggage from another camel to his back, and place the fresh one in the cart, which worked well.

We were travelling over an altitude of about 3000 feet; distance from Kalgan about 150 miles.

We were not able to get our usual supply of milk as we had seen no yourts to-day, and water was very scarce; we could only get enough to make some tea, so we had to go without our usual soup, having to content ourselves with a frozen tongue. Certainly, as far as we had gone, we had had splendid weather. Our hands got in an awful condition, cut, rough, and dirty, as our means for washing were very limited. All day we passed over a sandy flat plain, no vegetation whatever being visible. Although I have marked in my map places where villages are supposed to be situated, it is impossible to speak correctly of their whereabouts, as, for reasons I have before given, they are constantly changing. As we approached nearer the centre of the desert, for six or seven days we hardly saw even a single yourt; and again, as we approached the other side, we found traces of where villages had been, but which migrate every winter bodily to Urga. The plain we passed over to-day was thickly covered in parts with salt deposits. I tasted several of them, to be certain, and found them to be bitter and salt. We also found some very curious pebbles and petrifactions. One part, for about two miles, was strewn with camels' bones, and might well be called the Plain of the Dead, for nothing was seen but these ghastly skeletons. Whenever we made our usual halt huge ravens made their appearance, which was unpleasantly suggestive, as they were waiting for any death that might occur. We tried to drive them away, and shot one or two, but still they would come back; and whenever at night I put my head out of my cart I was sure to see one of these huge carrion birds keeping sentinel outside.

On the 2nd of November we experienced a slight foretaste of what a north-east wind is like in the desert of Gobi. The thermometer stood at 18°. I do not think that I ever felt so cold as I did that morning, not yet being hardened to it. The cold tea I carried with me, which I always made overnight, was frozen, and the bread like a brickbat—a bad look-out for us, as we had now no means of replenishing our stores, and supplies of fuel were very precarious. I had on a tight-fitting sheepskin coat and top-boots lined with fur, but with all this I could not face the wind; so, getting under every available wrap, and even putting my small carpet-bag over me in the cart, I smoked as hard as I could, which was all we got this day in the shape of food, and nothing but a small glass of sherry to drink. I must confess that home did appear to me very attractive, and hopes of ever getting there seemed " small by degrees and beautifully less." Thank goodness, towards evening the wind died away, and although it was awfully cold, still we were able to enjoy the clear still night, with a moon shining so brilliantly that it was easy to read by its light. Before retiring to rest as usual, our lamas informed us that there were *moo kung* (bad men) about this part of the desert. One always kept watch at such times; so it was arranged that in case of anything happening the lama was to give a sort of a cry, and we would be immediately ready with our revolvers. One of our camels having broken down, we had changed him, with the usual amount of bargaining, for another one ; so to-night we intended, as we also were glad to get a little more rest, waiting until twelve o'clock. The moon set at ten, and the wind gradually rose again. I could not sleep, as it penetrated through the cracks of the cart, sending clouds of sand through the windows. Although the moon had set, it was a clear night.

In these parts of the world, the atmosphere being so rarefied, makes even the darkest night appear tolerably clear. I have seen in the night objects even in the far distance. It is curious, though, in the day-time, how objects in the distance become magnified. A man on a camel looks like a hill, and a small dog like some gigantic animal. I have seen troops of Tartars riding along, looking like an advance of a line of poplar-trees; in fact, everything is very deceptive, and it is nearly impossible to calculate distances. You may enter a plain which looks, at most, ten miles across, and still, after travelling all day, find yourself a long distance from the slight elevations which indicate the end of the plain and the commencement of the next one.

It was about eleven o'clock, and nothing could be heard beyond the howling of the wind and the plaintive cry of our camels. Camels snore and dream. I often watched them when dreaming; they seem to suffer like dogs, with a similar sort of shiver and nightmare. Suddenly a cry broke from the tent where our Lamas were. We were both awake, and always being dressed, opened our carts at once. The camels were all on their haunches, about fifty yards from us, the tent being nearly between. I could just see two or three men or ponies near them, but hardly distinctly, on account of the tent. My friend's cart being behind mine, he could see what was going on better than I could.

A shot from his revolver made a sudden change in the scene, as instantaneously three figures on ponies scudded away across the plain. On approaching the camels, we found that two of them were unloosed; the method of keeping them down, or not allowing them to rise, being to tie the nose-string to the hump. These strings were loose; so, no doubt, our three robbing friends intended marching off with them if they had not been discovered. Although our Lamas had left it to us to frighten them away, I do not think if we had been asleep that they would have remained passive, as they were strong, courageous men, and well able to take care of their own. They, however, deemed it prudent for us to continue our march at once; so, all helping, we quickly struck our tent and hoisted our baggage, &c., on our camels, and proceeded onwards without delay.

We were henceforth impressed with the necessity of a strict watch at night, and whenever we fancied the Lama on watch was asleep, would shout out his name. We had christened, if I may use such a term, our two Lamas "Cocoanut" and "Monkey," as one resembled so much the fruit, the other the animal; and they were quite accustomed to these names, and used to call one another by them—of course not understanding their meaning. For instance, one of them being away, we would say, "Cocoanut," and then point, "Monkey;" and Cocoanut, for reply, would point to the horizon, and say, "Monkey;" so we knew he had gone ahead, either to visit some acquaintance or arrange about new camels.

As usual, we got no sleep during the night. I fancy our Lamas, who could sleep on their camels' backs as comfortably as if in a bed, did so during the nights, as we used to find ourselves in most curious places, and came to continual halts; and we were obliged to be constantly on the alert, shouting out their names to keep up our march. I am certain we travelled over much more ground than we need have done, as often at night we found ourselves going north-east, our proper course being north-west; and then we had to retrace our steps again, often too with much difficulty.

We found ourselves progressing in the language used amongst the Mongols, and could ask for a few necessary things; but it is most difficult, there being no way of properly learning it. The Mongols speak a distinct language from the Chinese, but they have little or no literature of their own, the characters used being Chinese. Very few amongst them, even of their Lamas, know how to read or write; having no postal communication amongst themselves, of course a written correspondence is entirely unknown, all communications between chiefs of clans or relatives being verbal. They are perfectly ignorant as to other countries, and probably the majority imagine that the world consists of Mongolia. Their religious ideas are hazy and undefined; however, they profess Bhuddism. Of course it is hard to understand such a perfect state of ignorance, but if happiness is a test of goodness, certainly these people prove the old proverb which says, " Where ignorance is bliss 'tis folly to be wise."

On the 3rd of November the cold was still increasing, the thermometer marking 9°, or 23° of frost. The north-east wind was sweeping across the plain, which was becoming terribly monotonous to us. I would have given anything to have seen a tree, or even a little grass, and much to have come across some good water, which we were rather in want of. The only thing that could be done was to walk all day. Eating was out of the question until we halted, as everything was hard frozen. I tried to ride on my now docile pony, but it was too cold. Our unfortunate ponies were looking very miserable and becoming footsore, and we determined to get rid of them as soon as possible, for it seemed cruel taking them further in the desert, as all chances of finding fodder or water were daily becoming less. During the afternoon we passed over a rocky country, ascending a little, the altitude reaching over 4000 feet; this was a change, but it jolted our carts and contents about sadly. Halting at half-past four at the foot of some rocks which afforded a shelter from the wind, I attempted to wash my face and hands, but was soon discovered in a frozen and melancholy condition by one of our Mongols, and taken helplessly by him into the hut and thawed before the fire, from which process I suffered for two hours afterwards the most exquisite pain; I am sure, however, if I had not been discovered, I should, something like Lot's wife, have been turned into a pillar of ice, instead of salt. At 7 P.M. the thermometer stood at 2°, and was still going down, and giving indications of a stronger wind. I certainly did feel a wish that it were possible to go back, but that was quite out of the question. Nothing happened during the night, except that it was impossible to get any rest, the country we were passing over being so rocky, and the camels seeming to delight in taking us over about the worse pieces they could pick out. To our great delight we reached Tsagan Tugurik at 11.30 A.M., on the 4th. This was the first point we had reached from which we could at all judge where we were. It is magnificently designated a town; all we saw were a few miserable yourts—about six—and a little white temple and house recently built for the officiating priest. The temple is the smallest I have ever seen. What in the summer is evidently a grassy plain was now entirely dried up. The distance from Kalgan we made to be about 300 miles, which we had taken eight days to accomplish—very different from railway speed. There is said to be a lake about here, but we could not find any trace of it, although we remained some time in order to find it. We felt quite cheered up at reaching this place, as we were feeling rather anxious and depressed before; but knowing we were travelling in the right direction and getting over the ground did us much good.

Sending our caravan ahead, we rode to a yourt and procured some first-rate milk. We visited all the yourts, but could not help saying, " Fancy this being called a town!" The plain was covered with camels, I should fancy at least 1000 of them— all looking in fine condition. Our Lamas, who had friends here, evidently wished to make a halt, but to this we objected, as every hour was now of consequence. We did not desire a longer residence in the desert than possible, and we still calculated on fifteen days at least longer, before reaching Kiachta. After leaving Tsagan Tugurik we proceeded over a rocky country for about two miles, and then across a succession of plains covered with snow about a foot thick, but hard frozen; but we were now assured we could always get water. We encamped at five on a small patch of sand with a little grass on it, which our animals soon disposed of.

A whole family of Mongols, consisting of five girls, the father, and mother, came from a neighbouring yourt, and all squatting down on their haunches round our tent, watched us preparing our dinner, the girls assisting us by keeping up the fire; we made an extra quantity of soup, so we shared it with them, and gave them a few ten-cent pieces, with which they were delighted. The girls, especially the eldest, were fine, healthy, and good-looking, ranging from about fourteen to twenty-two. Some of our fur coats sadly wanted repairing, which one of the girls, with a huge wooden needle, set to work to accomplish, being highly delighted at the task, the mother and father evidently pleased at their daughter's skill. They jabbered most incessantly, and seemed quite satisfied when we nodded our heads. It really was an interesting sight; all sitting round our tent, a fire blazing in the centre, outside ice and snow, and and the camels all huddled together, we dressed in our long sheepskin mantles and high fur hats, one of the girls working, another one feeding the fire, and my travelling companion stirring the soup, and occasionally tasting it. I felt quite comfortable. After dinner the whole family trooped off, and left us again to our solitude. We were just retiring to rest when an old Mongol, about sixty years of age, came galloping down at a great pace to our tent, intending to pay us a visit. We were just taking a little drop of whisky, but as our supply was getting very limited we did not care about parting with any. No sooner did our ancient friend see it than he intimated a desire to have some ; but we knew if we gave to one we should probably be bothered all night, several yourts being near us. So we thought to give him a dose which would stop any further applications. We produced a large bottle of cayenne pepper, the effect of which our friend never dreamt of. Giving him in the palm of his hand as much as would cover a threepenny piece, we made signs to him to lick it up, which he did immediately. The effect was instantaneous; for, with a howl, he jumped on his horse, and we nearly died with laughter as we saw him wheeling and whooping away in the distance. However, our Lamas, who had enjoyed the joke as much as we did, advised us to start at once, as we might have an unpleasant invasion, as no doubt it would be thought that we had poisoned the old Mongol.

We proceeded along at a good pace, for, although our Lamas, whenever they made signs to us as of licking up pepper were convulsed with laughter, they were evidently very much afraid of the consequences. We had purchased enough fuel to last us for at least two days, the Lamas paying for it in millet, a supply of which we to-day discovered they carried with them for the purpose. Our Lamas only had one meal a day, as we did, but the quantity they took at one time was enormous. Whenever we passed a yourt one of them would ride up to it, and in return for his blessing would, if a sheep was killed, be presented with the entrails, which they would cook at night. We calculated that each of them on these festive occasions ate at least five pounds weight. It was a too disgusting sight to see them gorging, so whenever they commenced we used to beat a hasty retreat to our carts.

On the 5th we rose from our carts at six, the thermometer stood at 2°, and it was bitterly cold. During the night we had passed over some deep snow-drifts, which very much impeded our progress, but about 7 A.M. we left the plain and entered into a hilly country, very barren indeed, and yourts became scarce. The roads were also excessively rough. We fared badly this day, as we could get neither water nor milk, and all our provisions were frozen. At twenty minutes before three, we saw a most curious phenomenon: three suns, most distinctly, in the sky. So much were they alike that it was impossible to distinguish which was the true one. All three were shining brightly. It lasted until half-past four, one alternately fading away and appearing, until they finally set together. Our Lamas informed us, with many grave shakes of their heads, that this was a bad sign, and that we should soon have a gale; which unfortunately came true. The three Chinese Mongols, who had stuck to us up to this time, much against our will, had become so obnoxious to us for their pilfering and other disagreeable propensities, that we intimated pretty plainly we should not allow them to accompany us any longer. They were constantly asking either for eatables or something or other, with a perseverance which was most annoying. At last, finding one of them coolly helping himself to a biscuit I had left in my cart, I presented my revolver at him; and then we intimated, that if they did not leave us at once we should proceed to force. I think our Lamas, who also now saw that two would fare better than five, also added their authority to ours; for after a great deal of angry altercation, and I believe a great deal of abuse especially devoted to us, they rode ahead on their camels, and we gradually lost sight of them. However, I have a suspicion that during the next two nights they joined us again for a time, but we saw no more of them.

We had to discourage all hangers-on, as it was quite enough trouble to keep stores for our own wants, and we could not afford to dispense them to others. During the night a strong north-west wind commenced rising, and towards morning increased into a gale. These winds are more feared than any others by the natives, as the force they attain to is almost incredible. Camels cannot even stand against them. Whirlwinds of sand and stone accompany them. Our Lamas intimated that if the wind increased we should have to stop, and were it not that we were afraid of establishing a precedent we should have been only too delighted to order a halt at once, for anything so horrible I never experienced. All my windows being broken I had to stuff my pillows in the frames, but this was but a poor support against this awful wind. The phenomenon we had seen, foreshadowed only too truly our Lamas' fears. Towards noon the violence of the gale somewhat abated, but the cold was intense. Having nothing to drink we suffered a good deal, as the sand had penetrated into our hair, eyes, and mouth, and even a few biscuits were nearly uneatable, being so full of sand, &c. We managed however at about twelve o'clock to get a little milk, which if we had not obtained

I much think we should have found it difficult to go on, for we were utterly exhausted and parched.

How delightful it is, after having undergone intense suffering, to feel an alleviation of it! And how soon it is all forgotten! It changed our whole thoughts, and we felt again hopeful, and began to enjoy the track we were passing over, which was much better and smoother. Pasture land also was becoming more abundant although all the grass was dried up. I calculated the distance from Tsagan Tugurik to be about 120 miles. We now proceeded over a plain covered with different sorts of pebbles glittering in the sun like precious stones. They were transparent and of all colours and shapes, and amongst them lots of flints and fine agate. We also discovered remains of petrifaction; which is a proof that formerly this portion of the globe was under water, and has since, by some convulsion of nature, been raised to its present elevation. We had never been, since we came into the desert, under 3000 feet, and at times we had travelled over ground 4000 feet and more, above the sea's level. It is a marvellous thing, finding a plain, standing as it does, in the centre of a continent, larger than England and nearly uninhabited.

We passed over some very remarkable looking

hills during the day which were decidedly volcanic. We discerned lava, which would prove that volcanic action must have occurred here at some previous period. We also noticed plenty of ironstone, copper ore, and slate, near the surface, imbedded in the sand. Mongolia would be a grand field for a geologist. To-day we camped near some yourts, and of course had to receive the various inhabitants who came to stare at us. At one time we had eighteen in our tent, which, not being large, rather limited us for space. What seemed to astonish them was to watch us eating our soup with spoons—an excess of refinement unknown amongst them; their method being to dip a wooden saucer in the caldron and haul out lumps of meat with their fingers and then consume it in a second, without mastication. We never allowed fingers to dip into our saucepan until we had filled our bowls, after which we handed the remainder to our Lamas, who disposed of it like a couple of dogs in the twinkling of an eye. Thinking that, as we received all these visitors, we would return their calls, we wandered round in the dusk, to the nearest yourts, stopping at each a short time, and partaking of an awful compound called tea (but which tasted more of its principal ingredient, mud, than of that pleasant leaf,) and kept up a mild conversation with the few words we now knew. We could not help enjoying their excessive innocence, and I may say ignorance. Producing our watches, we told them to blow upon them three times; at the third blow we pressed the spring and of course the watch opened, much to their wonder and delight, as they knew nothing about the spring, and firmly believed the three blows did the business. We had to repeat this to some twenty of them, and I never shall forget their astonishment; they had never seen a watch before, and were quite ignorant of its use. The ticking also pleased them, especially the women. Their method of calculating time is by the sun; but I never could discover if they have any time or dates, to correspond with ours. A long six-bladed knife I had, created immense excitement, especially a saw blade; to possess it I have no doubt they would have given me anything they had; but the climax was reached when, producing our revolvers, we got one of the young Mongols to put his hat upon a stick, and we sent two bullets through it. We offered to let them examine them, but not one of them would touch them, and they all took care to keep clear of the muzzles. This was good for us, as although we had no fear of the natives, still it created an effect and would be sure protection to us.

We had a flask with us, out of which we gave a little brandy to the people we visited. When we proceeded to our encampment we were accompanied by the whole tribe, and as we were not going to move for another three hours we invited the male portion into our tent, and produced two bottles of whisky, a recklessness of extravagance which we repented before long. Most of them would only taste a small quantity, but two old fellows, Lamas, I regret to say, we egged on, plying them with the liquid, which they drank off. They drank a bottle of pure spirit between them, at least. As the fumes mounted to their brains they sang and yelled frantically. I shall never forget it, and how we laughed. At last, however, the bottles being empty, the sons of these now very drunk old Lamas got them up, and we could hear them shouting away as they reeled home. I am afraid the next day's headache must have made them curse our memory. Our Lamas seemed very much scandalised, but I had seen them also quietly partake of a drop when they thought we were not looking.

Two of the Mongols, before bidding adieu, presented us each with a curious snuffbox, a small agate bottle with a little wooden spoon in it. In return, we gave them each a new Hong Kong dollar, which no doubt they will keep as we shall also do their present, as a relic of a very amusing evening.

CHAPTER IV.

How the Mongols cure a Camel's cracked Hoof — The Tartar Village of Wyshan — Great Dwelling-place of Lama Priests — The Country for a Railroad, from Russia to China — My Camel becomes untied from our Train, and I am left alone in the Night in the Desert, without Food — Cocoanut returns and finds me — A Lot of Marmots — A Plateau surrounded with Rocky Mountains — Herds of Ponies, Camels, and wild Gurush — Provisions running scarce, we purchase a Sheep of some Mongols — A Difficulty in killing him — We kill a wild Gurush — Signs of the End of the Desert — Notwithstanding our Hardships, our Retrospect a pleasant one — The way I kept Time — A Storm of Sand and Stones — We visit a Yourt, to warm ourselves — The half-breed Mongols bad characters — As my Head is bald I am taken for a Lama — Camels without Water for Ten Days — My Experience as to the Kind of Cart to travel with — We descend into a deep Valley — A Russian knocks us up at Night, a sign we were getting near our Journey's End — The North-east Wind nearly freezes us to our Carts — An Obon — A magnificent Prospect of Rocky Crags at our Feet.

SHORTLY after ten o'clock we proceeded again on our way; the wind had gone down, so we managed to get a little sleep during the night, the track being better. Towards morning we had to make a short halt, as one of our camels had a cracked foot, which, unless immediately attended to, would have rendered him lame and useless. The mode of cure is singular. The camel is made to kneel down and then the nose-string is tied to the hump. The Lama then makes a rush at it and over it goes on its side; another Lama then sits on its head. After a slight struggle, and shrieking like a child, the camel, with dismal groans, gives into its fate, and then the Lama sows a thick piece of leather, with a leather thong, across the crack. This only partially effects a cure, as the camel never does much good afterwards unless turned out to graze, in order that the foot may heal properly.

Considering the amount of work camels do, making a steady march every day of eighteen hours without halting, and getting no food or water, they certainly are remarkable animals, and so patient and docile. When a camel is required to work well it is kept very sparingly. I always noticed that whenever we purchased a new one it was very fat, and if any fodder was to be found, which was seldom the case in the desert, it was not allowed for a day or two to have any. The distance máde this day was about thirty miles.

On the 7th, at 7·30 A.M., the thermometer stood at 14°; it was a brilliant day, and towards noon it became quite warm, the thermometer reaching to 28°, but still not high enough to thaw the contents of my cart. Nevertheless, it was most enjoyable to us to bask in the sun after the horrible cold we had been experiencing. At ten o'clock we passed Wyshan, a Tartar village; distance from Tsagan Tugurik about 200 miles. It consisted of a group of yourts towards the western side, painted red, and a few wooden buildings on the east side of the road; this is the great dwelling-place of Lama priests. There is a large monastery, where they are educated. From all we could learn, there are at times from two to three thousand monks here. Of course it was necessary for our Lamas to pay a few visits here, so we halted a short time to suit them, and endeavoured to find water, which however was so bad that we could not drink it. It cannot help striking the traveller what a country it would be for a railroad, which would speedily make it the direct route from Europe to China, as it is nearly flat; engineering difficulties, beyond a few cuttings, would hardly be found. The only difficulty would be fuel and water, but still enough could be carried to last two or three days : a sufficient time for an easy journey from Pekin to Urga. The traffic between China and Kiachta, already very large, would be enormous. Hardly a day passed without our overtaking or meeting caravans consisting of two or three hundred camels, laden with tea for Russia or produce for China. A caravan takes at least forty days to accomplish the journey. I cannot help thinking that one of these days this must be the direct route to China. With a railroad through Siberia, and a line from Urga to Pekin, it could be done in a very short time, compared to the now long voyage by the overland route, so called, which, instead of being overland, with the exception of Egypt, is all by sea. To-day we had been gradually ascending until we encamped at 5 P.M. on an altitude of 4000 feet. The reason the cold is so great in Mongolia is no doubt because the plain is situated so much above the sea level. The country here becomes much more interesting; vast undulating plains extend on all sides as far as the eye reaches. Hills in front, and the grass, which was however much dried up, becomes plentiful.

During the day we saw several herds of wild *gurush*, and I had three shots with my rifle at them at 900 yards' distance, and succeeded each time in sending a bullet in the centre of the herd, but unfortunately without result. These animals resemble small deer, and are excessively timid, and scented our approach long before we could get near them. However we were very much pleased to see them, as we now anticipated some good sport, and something to while away the monotony of the journey. I had tried my rifle with success at large birds, and sent a bullet through a small stick at 200 yards, but unfortunately ammunition was getting scarce.

We encamped at the foot of a small pass, having made since last night about forty miles—a good day's work. Starting again at 10 P.M., we proceeded over the pass, reaching 4600 feet, and then found ourselves in a plain again. I was very tired and done up, so managed to sleep before we started, and was not awakened by the usual process of harnessing in, or even by the jolting we were getting, over the very rough track we were passing over, being now somewhat hardened to it. Our Lamas, who got very little regular sleep, generally took it out on the backs of their camels, and a very awkward adventure resulting therefrom happened to me during the night, which deterred me from ever again sleeping comfortably until we reached Kiachta. Our general method of proceeding at night was, first rode one of the Lamas, on a camel, holding the nose-string of the camel harnessed into my friend's cart; then came all the baggage camels, followed by my cart, and, lastly, the other Lama brought up the rear. This was all right; but the two Lamas, I suppose for company's sake, rode ahead, and as we were both asleep when we started we knew nothing about it. For reasons I have before stated, the camels are loosely tied together, and easily come unstrung. I must have been asleep some time, for, waking about one o'clock, I missed the usual jolting about, and began to realise the fact that the cart was not in motion. Hastily opening the door, and looking all round, I discovered that I was in the midst of a large plain, entirely alone, the caravan, not aware of my being left behind, having gone quietly along. Vainly did I shout out for my travelling companions, and the names of our guides; they were far out of hearing, being already out of sight. As I began to realise my situation I must confess I felt extremely unhappy. There were plenty of wild animals about, and my camel, who was eating all he could find, had strayed far away with the cart out of the track, and even when they did discover my loss it is uncertain whether, even if they could retrace their way, they would find me. All our provisions had gone on, so I had also the pleasant prospect of being starved. If any wandering tribe of Tartars should have come down and found me all alone they would have been intensely surprised, especially as I could not speak to them, and the result would have been perhaps fatal to me. Fancy them finding a stranger seated in a cart, all alone in the midst of the desert, not knowing at all how he had got there! I looked about anxiously for traces of a track that the caravan must have passed over, but could find none, so it was evident that during my sleep the camel had wandered far out of it. To make matters worse, that perverse animal insisted now on lying down, so all I could do was to wait quietly in hope, so as not to attract attention.

It was only when I had given up all hopes and was beginning to resign myself to my fate, that to my intense delight, at four o'clock, I could just discern a figure on a camel in the horizon, which proved to be one of the Lamas. He had been searching for me for some time, and had nearly given up the pursuit; and unless he had discovered me then would have gone on again. It is very difficult to find at any time the route across the desert, as there are no traces, at least we never could see any wheel or foot-marks, or signs of them. When Cocoanut rode up to me he seemed delighted; but I was so exhausted that I only climbed into my cart, leaving him to raise the camel and proceed onward. I, however, poured forth my wrath on him later on. After a march of five hours we caught up the caravan, which was waiting for us. I found my travelling companion in a great state of anxiety, as he had only discovered that I was missing a short time before, and felt as helpless as I did, and of course did not know what steps to take. He awoke, and finding that the caravan had halted, as the usual custom between us was, he shouted out for me, and receiving no reply he soon discovered the state of affairs, and found that one of the Lamas had gone off in search of me. We henceforth determined to have our two carts in the centre, and keep, as far as we could, a watch all night. This, of course, delayed our march; but it was now daylight, so we proceeded on at once, feeling very thankful that it had turned out as well as it had. We saw a quantity of marmots on our way. They are droll little animals. They generally sat on their haunches until we came quite near, then, looking round at us, they would suddenly disappear into their holes. All the prairies round we found covered with the holes they burrow, and some of them very deep. Feeling very restless and excited after last night's adventure, I got out of my cart; it was about 7·30 A.M. I could see that we were on a vast plain. The thermometer was 16°, the sun had not yet risen, but the grey dawn made all things distinguishable.

There was no wind, so it felt pleasant. Soon the sun rose, like a large ball of fire coming out of the plain, and a truly glorious sight it was. We were on what seemed a boundless tract of undulating grassy prairie, covered with white frost, which, as the sun rose, looked like one vast expanse of glittering crystals, of all hues and colours. As the day increased we could more clearly perceive that we were on a table-land, surrounded on all sides by rocky mountains. Herds of ponies and camels were quietly grazing, and here and there flocks of wild gurush, but too distant for us to attempt to shoot them. Taking the whole scene, reflected as it was by the rays of the ruddy sun, pebbles glistening under foot, and the stars still shining in the clear blue sky, herds of animals in all directions, and the boundless extent of ground, it was a scene that I cannot describe. I soon felt refreshed by the clear bracing air, and soon forgot the predicament I had been in during the night, recalling it only to laugh over the absurd position I had been left in. We determined to-day to stalk some of the gûrush, and discover if it were not possible to bag one or two of them.

Provisions were becoming very scarce, our stock being reduced to a frozen tongue, a small piece of beef, and a few biscuits and vegetables; so we looked out anxiously for a yourt, where we might be able to purchase a sheep. About 11 A.M. we came across one, and found flocks of fine sheep, which incited us to business at once; and after a good deal of bargaining, through our Lamas, we purchased a whole animal for some broken silver, equivalent to about six shillings. This, however, did not include the killing and preparing the animal, and had we not insisted on the fact of our being Lamas—it not being allowed for them to touch blood—we should have had to slaughter and skin the sheep ourselves—an operation which we neither of us felt competent or willing to do. One of the family thereupon, for a small quantity of brick tea, undertook the job; so leaving one of our men to bring on the carcass, when ready, on his camel, we proceeded onwards. Passing over a succession of plains, each finishing with an ascent, where we expected, but were continually disappointed, to see something new, at about half a mile's distance we came across a fine herd of gurush. These we determined to get at, in some way or other. No sooner, however, did they catch sight of us than away they sped over the plain and disappeared over the ridge in front, descending into the next valley. This suited us well. My friend, with a Colt's revolver, mounted on his pony and rode round towards the end of the valley we were passing through, so as to cross the ridge far down and so drive them up the next valley, to the other end of which I walked on. Our plan succeeded famously; for no sooner had I reached the summit of the grassy hill ahead than I perceived my friend firing his revolver, as he headed down the valley, pursuing the whole flock, which were rapidly approaching towards the hill under which I was taking shelter; so, lying down, I waited until they should pass. On they came, but suddenly paused, sniffing danger; but my friend, who was about 500 yards behind, was closing on them, so on they came again. As they passed I picked out two, and fired rapidly, being rewarded by seeing one fall dead; the other, being only slightly wounded, escaped. This was something like fun! We found these animals to be very similar to the antelope, perhaps rather smaller, but not good eating, having a very peculiar flavour. Our Mongol who was with us was in a great state of excitement, and when Cocoanut arrived with the sheep, which looked a very unpleasant sight, slung across the camel, he related our exploit to him, which caused Cocoanut to repeat the word *sign*, which means "good," with great wonderment, at close intervals, for at least two hours afterwards. We were rather glad we had succeeded, as, after our continual failures, I believe our Lamas before this rather looked upon our shooting as a myth. We continued to pass herds of these animals, but could not again get near enough, and we did not care about wasting more ammunition, as it was becoming scarce. We had been continually asked on the way for powder, but we never gave any away. Some of the Mongols possess a sort of a gun, with a long barrel; it goes off with a fuse. I remember once, in China, seeing a soldier being taught to fire off a similar weapon, but larger—what is generally called a gingal. Closing his eyes he pulled the trigger, and then waited, with evident trepidation, for the fuse to

K

ignite the powder in the pan; which no sooner happened than up went the barrel in the air, and over he went. This operation he performed several times, to his own disgust as well as to his instructor's, who however was too wary himself to practically instruct his pupil. They are the most barbarous inventions; but I have seen Chinamen, with a long light similar weapon, make good practice at snipe. We were travelling over an altitude of 3800 feet, and about 4 P.M. we ascended gradually to over 5000. Grass becomes here more abundant, but still not a sign of a tree, which we would have given much to see, as a proof that we were getting nearer to Urga. We both remarked here that we never thought we could have stood the cold so well as we had done, coming direct from the south of China. But in this wonderful climate, where the air is so pure and bracing, and with the continual exercise, abstemious living, and even hardships, it is impossible to feel otherwise than in perfect health, which it is certain that, when God created man, he meant him to enjoy, and which he seldom does enjoy where civilisation exists.

I believe natives, in these parts, are rarely troubled with illness or disease, and I do not think that medicine or its administrators are known here.

The only troublesome part of the climate is that it made us so very hungry. When we could not sufficiently satisfy the appetite, I felt as if I could eat anything. I often was glad to break my teeth with a loaf of frozen bread.

Our unfortunate ponies were daily becoming not only more useless, but also a burden to us, as at times we could not get them to advance, and so were constantly retarded in our progress; although latterly we had been travelling over grassy plains, which gave them plenty of fodder, they had no water, for with the exception of a little snow we had come across during the last few days, we had none ourselves; and besides, the marching for eighteen hours a day was too much for them. My animal was becoming also quite footsore. How different he looked from the fiery little Tartar steed he was when I first purchased him! He had not now a kick in him. We determined to sell them as soon as we could, otherwise to abandon them at Urga. Coming across a tribe of Tartars during the day, we endeavoured without success to make a bargain. I believe they did not understand what we wanted, only thinking that we wanted to buy some more, so we gave it up as a bad job.

I am sure our Mongols would have been glad to

be rid of them, as, besides leading the camels, they had also to lead the ponies. On one occasion Cocoanut, being fast asleep on his camel, with the pony's halter tied round his arm, received a sudden abasement, finding himself on the ground, the pony having come to a sudden halt and pulled him out of his saddle, he nearly at the same time breaking his camel's nose. I am sure we could have done well without the ponies, for, with a few exceptions, when we rode ahead to yourts, they were of no use to us, it being much too cold to ride, and we generally walked eight to ten hours a day. We calculated, when we reached Kiachta, that we had walked at least 400 miles. Still proceeding over the plain we had entered in the morning, which looked only about six or seven miles across, we came into a more mountainous district, and now began to look forward to a decided change in the scenery and features of the country. The desert, so far as utter sterility is concerned, certainly finishes here; for although there is no sign of cultivation, or of vegetation of any sort, there is some grass, which, doubtless, in summer months is very abundant. We could see boundless prairies stretching forth on all sides, resembling much those found in America. Of course, there being no cultivation, bread and vegetables are commodities unknown amongst the Mongols. Amongst our stores we had taken with us a sack of bread ; we used to give a loaf occasionally to our Lamas, and it was most amusing to see them endeavouring to eat it. Besides being stale, it was hard frozen, and the grimaces they made were very curious. I believe they thought it was the natural state of bread, and wondered much what we found good in it. However, *experientia docet.* We afterwards discovered that by soaking the bread and then putting it before the fire, we managed to make it eatable.

Still in the plain. We encamped at half-past four, the distance made since last evening being about twenty miles. We made out, according to our usual method of communicating with our Lamas by the fingers, that it is possible, if all goes well, that we may reach Urga in three days, and Kiachta in eight; if so, we shall have made a very quick journey across. I cannot, up to the present, speak in too high praise of our Lamas, who have behaved very well and given us no trouble whatever. Should any one be crossing the desert and by chance obtain these guides he would no doubt be astonished to find them adepts in the art of cooking chops and even in making soup, we having taught them to do so, and equally surprised to hear them addressing each other by the names we had given them. Tonight they had a grand feast on the entrails of the sheep, eating until they were perfectly gorged, taking in one mouthful what would have served two ordinary men for a meal. We stipulated, however, that they should not commence even to cook their food until we had finished our dinner. We then just waited to see the commencement; but the sight was too disgusting, and soon obliged us to seek our carts. The new moon made its appearance, but the wind, our dreadful enemy, was getting up again, and the thermometer was gradually falling to zero. Writing in my cart, with my Chinese lantern hanging alight in the centre, some hot whisky by me, I endeavoured, but with small success, to cover myself well against the wind. Notwithstanding this wretched condition, looking back, I did so with pleasure, and even though the hardships had been great and this awful wind penetrated and chilled me to the bone, I would not have missed the journey through the desert on any account.

I will here mention a method I had of keeping dates and days. I wrote down in a fly-leaf of my diary three months with dates and days. Every evening I scratched out one, and placed the readings of thermometer and barometer against it. For some time this plan worked well; later on, in Siberia, however, by omitting once or twice to make the erasure, we occasionally lost count of days and dates. The sun set this evening about four o'clock and was a glorious sight, and unless seen our description would not be believed. The wonderful colours, like the aurora borealis, which illumined the atmosphere, were so intense as to render it impossible to gaze on the changing hues without experiencing a temporary blindness. As these changing colours faded, the deep blue sky, in which each simple star shone brightly enough to light up the darkness, appeared, and then the moon arose, lighting up the scene as clearly as the sun could have done. The falling stars are splendid, like comets. I have seen some dart through the heavens, leaving a long tail behind, which took two or three minutes before it disappeared. Another feature is the frozen humidity in the air; which falls like glittering spangles, as they were during the evening illumined by the moon.

We proceeded onwards again at 10 P.M. The track being too rough, as was usually the case at night, I could not sleep; and besides, last night's mishap prevented me also from doing so, keeping me in a continual state of fidget. Whenever we stopped, even for a few moments, to allow the Lamas to find the track, I always fancied I was again lost and being left behind. I never got rid of this impression until I finally bade adieu to my cart at Kiachta. On the morning of the 9th, when I got out of my cart it was to be nearly thrown over by a north-east wind, which went right through me. We could not walk against it, and moreover, the clouds of sand and stones were becoming intensely annoying and nearly made us blind. We were unable to proceed, so for the first time since we started, encamped at 11 A.M., and turned our tent's back to the wind. Although we did not like to confess it, and, consequently, appeared to our Lamas to be much vexed at this delay, fearing it was a precedent which should not be established, we were glad to get sheltered somewhat from the wind. Besides being frozen and half suffocated with sand we were quite exhausted, and the strongest constitution would not hold out much longer against the fearful gale we had been facing since ten last evening. Two of the camels were quite done up and refused to proceed, one of them looking in a dying condition, and there were no signs of camels near us; so we were in a fix and uncertain what to do. Cocoanut, however, left us in search, promising to return as soon as possible.

We were encamped in a large plain; on our right were some lofty mountains, called the Rich Mountains, probably on account of metals being found in them. There was also plenty of snow and ice about, so we had water in abundance. The thermometer stood at 2° above zero. As we determined to start again so soon as Cocoanut should return, we pitched our tent, lighted our fire, and prepared our usual one meal per day, eating as much as we could, to tide us over until next day at 5 P.M. We also bottled some soup; however, we might have saved ourselves the trouble of doing this, as it froze very soon afterward, and only rendered our bottles useless. We hardly ever got anything to drink except when we halted, and not always then. Seeing a yourt near us, after dinner we proceeded to it, taking some chocolate, in case we could obtain some milk to boil it with. Putting aside the felt door we entered, but found no one at home, not even the inevitable dog, an animal which we generally found in all the yourts, and so watchful that no amount of persuasion would prevent him from attempting to bite us; an endeavour which generally ended in the dog being tied down by the head to a stake during our stay. We blew up the fire, which was smouldering, and over which was the usual caldron with snow water in it, and proceeded to boil it, so as to make our chocolate. Whilst engaged in this operation the inevitable dog, who had evidently not been far off, sniffed us out, and we had the pleasure of seeing him pushing under the door. No sooner had he done this than he commenced a most savage onslaught on us, which we had great trouble in repelling, the yourt being too low to allow us to stand upright. I think the battle would have gone against us, as we had no sticks, it being considered a sign of great discourtesy to bring one into a yourt, when the owner, a very ancient dame, with a basket full of argolots in her hand, entered, and looked very much astonished to see us; but she soon called off the dog and tied him down, so we could only hear the sullen grunt of that indignant but unconquered animal.

A smiling countenance, the usual greeting, and a few small coins, soon produced a hearty welcome, and the ancient dame, busily making up the fire, chattered incessantly, not waiting for our answers, which, as we had none to give, relieved us of attempting an impossibility. She very much liked the chocolate, so we gave her a small supply. Feeling warmed and better we bade our old friend adieu, and shaped our way to our tent again. It was now 3 P.M., and we anxiously looked for Cocoa-nut, but as yet there was no sign of him. The violence of the wind had increased; our tent was swaying about, and required double stays to keep it from being carried bodily away ; the fire was extinguished, and the shades of evening were coming on. To make things worse, a storm of sleet also came on. Vainly did we endeavour to get warm, and dreary seemed the prospect before us. It is a wonder to me, now that I am comfortably seated in a warm room writing this, how we did manage to survive the fearful discomfort these storms brought on us Unless any one has experienced these winds in the desert, from which there is no protection, he cannot imagine their fearful intensity. The only thing we could do was to retreat into our carts, and wrap up as well as our benumbed fingers and hands would let us; but all the furs, blankets, &c., were of little use. Certainly our carts were back to the wind. What it would have been, were we proceeding onwards with my three windows broken I dare not contemplate. Monkey having nothing to do, with his assistance I managed to nail some felt over the frames, which, however, excluded all daylight, but only a small portion of the wind. Seven o'clock, and still no signs of Cocoanut with new camels. I half believe it is a ruse of our head Lama, as he has been entertaining various friends of his, who have galloped up to the tent during the last two hours at intervals, from suspiciously near distances. I expect that Cocoanut has gone off to some feed or other, alleging the difficulty of procuring camels as an excuse. If we find it to be so, Messrs. Monkey and Cocoanut will suffer in a pecuniary point of view for keeping us a whole day longer in this inclement country.

I must say here that the charms of the Mongol natives had somewhat worn off. Perhaps I am describing feelings rather aggravated by the cold winds; but the more one sees of the caravan Mongols the less one likes them. Of course there are many exceptions. I am speaking as a general rule. They are always asking for spirits or money, or something, and among them there are some very bad characters. These are not however pure Mongols, but half Chinese. There are many who drink a large quantity of noxious spirit like arrack, and very rank stuff it is. I am afraid our Lamas tell them we have whisky; hence the continual bother for it. The Lamas have their heads shaven close and wear no tail. I always pass for one, as unfortunately my hair is getting scant at the top. We find all through the regions we have been passing that yourts are becoming very scarce and far between, as upon the first approach of winter most of the inhabitants pack up their tents, and with their families and herds migrate to Ta-Kurin, or Urga, and take up their abode there, returning again into the wilderness in spring. During our stay to-day another of our camels underwent the process of having a leathern patch sewn over his foot. I do not think that any of our animals have had water for ten days. The ponies, who have been making the best of the halt, seem much better, so much so that when I approached mine this evening he lashed out at me, and bolted away at a fine pace.

Cocoanut returned at last, at 11 A.M., so he had wasted a great many hours, and although we felt it our bounden duty to appear very angry, really at heart we were very much pleased at the delay, as, for the first time for many nights, we managed to get sleep for a few hours. Cocoanut, who was always in good spirits, even under the most trying circumstances, when Monkey would become useless, was not at all put out at our venting our indignation at him, but, with his usual grunt—which intimated he had been spending a pleasant day—proceeded at once to make ready for proceeding on our journey, and loaded the new camels—which were first-rate animals, one of them being pure white—with our baggage. Another old Lama joined us, and intimated his desire to accompany us; but this we decidedly objected to, as besides being a dirty, disagreeable old man, our stores were scant, and not enough, we feared, to last us to Urga; however, we could hear him jabbering away with our men, so no doubt he attempted to proceed during the night with us. These old Lamas, when wanting to travel, leave such material things as provisions, &c., to Providence, join the first caravan they see, and, for the blessing of their company—a blessing not always appreciated—accept being fed and sometimes even clothed. However, as we had no special reverence for these very dirty wanderers, we always stood out against any accessions of them.

We proceeded onwards, with incessant halts, my

camel evincing his dislike to drawing my cart by kicking violently, without any effect, as far as the cart was concerned, but with great detriment to his own legs, as after a time he gave up the trial as a bad job. At 5 A.M. we came to a halt again; the camels were taken out of the carts in a moment, and turned back to the wind, which was blowing fiercer than ever; we could only see we were halted on the brink of what seemed a precipice. Expostulations were in vain, as Monkey had disappeared this time; the usual excuse being given, that he had gone to get camels, and he was soon followed by Cocoanut; so we found ourselves left to our own reflections, entirely alone, with six camels and two ponies to look after. This was a bit of coolness we could not put up with; but what could we do? And if this sort of thing was to go on we might make up our minds to an indefinite sojourn in Mongolia. Besides, it was annoying, being the only real hitch we had had since we started, and the weather looked very bad. I am afraid I was premature in praising our Lamas; a little moral persuasion with a good thick stick, if we could have come across them just then, would have decidedly resulted from this last trick of theirs. I am persuaded the old Lama was at the bottom of it, as he took care to leave us before morning—one of our forks and a tin goblet going with him, which was an irreparable loss to us. Monkey, who I believe knew all about it, as he afterwards stole a fur cap of mine, declared we must have left them behind at the last halting-place. Luckily my travelling companion was fast asleep, and so in happy ignorance I heard him shout out, *Hordan jabo!* (go quickly); but as I did not hear him again I concluded he had slept again, under the impression that we were making rapid progress, and I had not the heart to awaken him. As I could not sleep—feeling very unsettled in my mind, not knowing where we happened to be, or indeed if our Lamas had left us in the lurch, and hence feeling the necessity of keeping watch— I lighted my lamp and my pipe, and, stuffing up every crack I could find in my cart, made myself as comfortable as I could. I certainly should have much liked to be able to drink the soup I had bottled, but it was too hard frozen; however, by this time we had both become too much accustomed to suffer hunger and thirst to grumble when we had nothing. I find recorded in my diary the following, written during this halt: "If I had ever to travel again through Mongolia, which may the Fates defend! I would have a light cart built, six feet long and four broad, with strong wooden springs. The inside should be well lined with felt, and should have good deep shelves all round, about one foot from the roof, and plenty of pockets; and I would only have one large glass window in front, with good strong shutters to it, in case of its breaking. I think the journey also could be done in much shorter time by taking mules on for three or four days—of course it would be necessary to carry sustenance for them—and so getting over 250 miles, or nearly a third of the journey; the camels to be sent on some days in advance, with all heavy baggage, to await the arrival of the carts and mules. More than this could not be done, as the cart could not carry enough fodder for those places where all grass ceases, and where there is but little water to be found. I would never travel with my own tent, as the Mongols who accompanied us always had one, which suits all purposes, for cooking, &c. It is much better to sleep in the cart, and thus save the trouble and loss of time of first putting one's bedding in the tent, and then, when starting again, having to transfer it to the cart; which, besides doing away with any chances of sleep, makes it very disagreeable in cold weather. Our rule was always to halt at 4 to 5 P.M., have our dinner, then retire into cart at 7 P.M., and read and smoke, and get as much sleep as possible until 10 or 11 P.M., when we started again; this, with the thermometer at zero and a north-east wind blowing, is much preferable to having to transfer the bedding from the tent to the cart."

We now looked forward to seeing the river Toll, which we have to cross before reaching Urga. This is generally looked upon as the most difficult part of the journey, as after snow or rain it becomes flooded and dangerous to ford, so we were somewhat anxious to reach it. However, there cannot have been much rain or snow lately, as we have, with one or two exceptions, experienced dry weather since we left Pekin, twenty-two days ago, although a great deal of snow must have fallen in some parts, considering the quantity we have passed over at various times. The ordinary Mongol hat, made of fur, provided us with a capital nightcap. Not that, as a rule, I wear that commodity, but when the wind is whistling through every crevice in a rotten old cart it wraps one's face up, like being in a bag, and keeps away all draughts. I cannot recommend it too strongly to the notice of any traveller who may find himself persuaded to undergo this journey, the greatest drawback of which is that it is much too long.

At 8 A.M. on the 10th, our Lamas having returned, we were all ready for a start again, and descended a rather steep incline, which the camels felt some difficulty in getting down. We calculated that we had lost at least a day by the various delays we had been put to latterly. Up to one o'clock we had continued to pass over a series of undulating grassy plains, covered with snow, and expecting as we reached the end of each of them to see something new. But as plain after plain appeared, and the north-east wind increased again, disgusted and weary we retired into our carts, with a vain endeavour to get warm. The thermometer was only 12°, but I often found it warmer with the thermometer several degrees below zero when there was no wind. At last, at one o'clock, all of a sudden, we found ourselves at an elevation of 3600 feet, at the brink of a rapid descent into a large valley surrounded with innumerable ranges of mountains. It was a splendid sight, and so new to us after our monotonous sixteen days in the desert.

The descent into the valley, however, was a matter of some difficulty, being very abrupt, and it was with many misgivings that we saw our camels and carts slipping and sliding over the snow; but we accomplished the descent in safety. Marching across the plain, with a bitter wind blowing, we reached the entrance to another larger valley at 6 P.M., where we encamped for the night. All the water about being frozen, we had to collect snow for our use. We could not yet discover any signs of trees, &c., on the mountains, but from the change in the aspect of the country, we expected shortly to reach the woods which we were to pass by before coming to Urga.

Certainly this evening, weary and hungry as we were, we found the innumerable Mongols who flocked in troops to our tents a nuisance. We had become by this time very tired of continually being made a sort of an exhibition of, and watched while we ate our daily meals. My travelling companion was a famous fellow, full of resources, as most Americans are, and always, notwithstanding the difficulties and hardships, in good spirits. I am convinced in a journey like this it is always better to travel only two together, as it is impossible to differ materially on any important point connected with the journey; three would be one too many, and four give rise to all manner of discussions and differences. We both began now to look forward to an early termination of our journey as far as Kiachta, and to wish most ardently that we were there, as going through a desert for sixteen days takes off the first novelty a bit, and makes one begin to think that there is a great deal too much of a good thing to be entirely agreeable. But still, notwithstanding the cold winds and various hardships, we both found ourselves better and stronger than when we started. Nothing like a similar journey to prove a man's constitution. To-day, being the birthday of Walcott's sister, we drank our last bottle of sherry, which reduced our liquids to a small quantity of whisky. To-night the moon shone brightly and the wind died away, so that, with the combined influence of the sherry, we felt tolerably comfortable. We still saw plenty of grouse by the way. Up to this time we certainly (with the exception of the wind) were most fortunate, having met with no rain and very little snow. The thermometer, however, never had been over 32° since leaving Kalgan.

We started again at 11 P.M., and as the way was not so rough I managed to snooze a bit, but was always afraid of being left behind. As I was getting into a sleep at about one o'clock I was awakened by some one tugging violently at my door ; but thinking it was some wandering Mongol, who probably when I had turned out of my warm coverings would only pester me for drink or something or other, which generally made me so angry that I was afraid of being tempted to shoot them, I remained quiet; so presently, after the door was nearly pulled off its hinges, the tugging ceased. But soon I heard my travelling companion, who had been aroused in the same manner, shouting out, and I understood him to say, "A ruffian is bothering me!" so only turning over, I shouted in reply, "Shoot him then!" The knocking and pulling at my door recommencing, I hastily got up, and, revolver in hand, opened the door, determined anyhow to make an example of the destroyer of my rest; but it proved to be a Russian, who, seeing me looking very angry with a revolver in hand, appeared rather alarmed. Whither he was bound or what he wanted, I could not make out at all. My travelling companion had sent him to me, as he could not understand him, and he thought that probably I could converse with him in German or French. However, these languages he was ignorant of, and he soon disappeared and we saw him no more. We were very sorry that our inability to speak with this stranger prevented us from gathering any information as to how far we were from Urga, and the nature of the country. He was the first approach to a European we had seen since leaving Kalgan, being a sort of a half-Mongol and half-Russian. Our Lamas, whose ideas were confined to Mongolia and Russia, seemed very much surprised that we were unable to understand Russian, and I think we fell in their estimation accordingly. After this of course all sleep vanished, so we got out of our carts and walked. We were gradually ascending into a hilly country, and early in the morning found ourselves 5000 feet over the sea-level. The scenery here was very wild, but, being quite barren, was not interesting. I have spoken much of the horrors of the wind we had experienced at times, but nothing we had yet gone through came up to what we experienced this well-remembered day. It was in vain we endeavoured by walking to induce circulation of the blood; such a hurricane was blowing, and showers of sleet, driving with fury against us, and cutting into our faces. The thermometer stood at 8°. Finding we could not endure the wind, we had to betake ourselves to the carts, but we were frozen. It was much too cold to think of eating some biscuits (which we were generally able to dispose of for lunch) with such a north-east wind blowing that it was nearly impossible to stand against it. Ice and snow were all round, clouds heavy and full of snow scudding away overhead, it would be impossible, if not felt, to realise the intensity the cold reaches. Nose, ears, fingers, and toes vanish, or seem to do so; for with the exception of a constant desire to blow one's nose, which, however, it is not easy to accomplish, as fingers are quite useless, all these members of the body become to all appearances dead. Finding the shelter the carts afforded even intolerable we hung on behind, putting on all our furs, and toiled along. In this manner, partially screened from the wind, we were at last rewarded by coming across a yourt, into which we hastily dived, and had a good warm by the fire and partook of some hot milk, after which, feeling much better, we proceeded to breast the storm. Still ascending, at 2 P.M. we reached a sort of a small table-land at the summit of a pass. The elevation, being 6800 feet, presented one of the grandest and finest spectacles that we saw during the whole journey. We stood for shelter behind a huge *obon*, our camels and carts being now far behind us; indeed, as we watched them toiling up, we had serious misgivings of their ever reaching the summit, every now and then one of the camels lying down and refusing to stir, and of course one of the Lamas had ridden off to see a friend, which one or other invariably did when most wanted.

I will here, with permission, describe an obon. At the summit of all the hills we passed we generally found one or more of them. They are generally pyramidal, and consist of stones, wood, &c., thrown by all Lamas, before descending the hill. Each as he passes throws a stone or piece of wood, or plucks a handful of hair from off his camel, on the obon, and so in time many of them attain to a large mass. This is done to propitiate the evil spirits who are supposed to dwell about these regions, without which it would be considered unsafe to commence the descent. Our Lamas finding us one day throwing some of the stones off an obon down a hill—we doing it in perfect ignorance— were horror-struck, and very unwilling to commence the descent; and if anything had happened of course they would have blamed us for the accident.

From whence we were standing, partly screened by the obon from the fury of the wind, we looked down a precipice into a valley surrounded on all sides by a sea of rocks, crags, and mountains, all jumbled together in confusion, as if some convulsion of nature had thrown them together pell-mell. Snow ridges to the right, called Tsagan, or White Mountains, attained to what seemed a great elevation even from where we were standing, and for the first time we could discern on the crests of some of the less lofty mountains small patches of fir trees. The sight was one not easily to be forgotten. Heavy clouds were drifting amidst the mountains and through the valley at our feet, here and there a gleam of the sun was resting on a rocky crag, and hills and rocks in all directions around. Although the wind was rapidly freezing us we could hardly tear ourselves away from this sight. It looked like a picture an artist might make as a subject for the infernal regions or the end of the world, so wild and so different was it from anything we had seen before.

CHAPTER V.

Our Provision Camel is lost, and Cocoanut goes in search of him—The other Camels refuse to descend the steep Incline, and the Ponies scamper off—Our remaining Guide goes to get Water, and we have to lead the Camels and Horses—Our remarkable Appearance in our Sheep-skin Clothing—Cocoanut and Monkey return again with the missing Camel—The Winter the best Season to do the Journey in—Pleasures of a free Life in the Desert—We cross the River Toll on the Ice—We reach the Chinese town of Mai-Mai-Chin—We visit the Russian Consulate—The Vice-Consul greets us with Delight—The only Europeans he had seen for a long time — We take leave of the Mongolian Desert here, and enter Siberia—Russia gradually encroaching upon the whole of Mongolia—Mai-Mai-Chin, the residence of the Lama King—Account of the Lama King, and his Method of Succession—We taste the Pleasures of Civilisation once more—We sell our Ponies here and start the same Day—An unpleasant Adventure in my Cart—We start against our Lama's Wishes—Oxen engaged to take us up the Mountain Pass—Queer Costume of the Female Driver—Perils of the Descent — We continue to ascend and descend.

WE now for the first time missed the camel which was laden with our baggage and provisions, and on inquiring into the matter found that Cocoanut—who had been absent some time, and who we thought was, as usual, visiting some friend or other—had gone in search of him. This rather dismayed us, especially when we found that the camel had strayed away the preceding night; and as we had no other baggage or provisions to depend upon if it were not found we should have been in a very awkward dilemma. The worst of it was that, by experience, we had come to the conclusion that our Lamas were, without exception, the most extraordinary liars (I believe, innocently, because they saw no fault in lying,) we ever came across, and it was impossible to believe any statement they made; and we feared that Cocoanut had decamped with the baggage. So we had only now one Lama to look after our two carts, five camels, and two ponies, and he in a state of helplessness from the cold. To make matters worse, we had a nearly perpendicular path, about 800 feet down, to descend, and all covered with hard snow. We had to tie up the wheels of our carts, but Monkey clearly was in a fix, for not a camel would stir, and so soon as ever a move was made one of them would get loose; this game went on for some time, when he lost all patience, let go the ponies' halters, and made signs to me to take charge of them, while my fellow-traveller helped to urge the camels on. But once the ponies finding themselves loose, it was all very well for me to attempt to get at them again, but as I approached, with a flourish of their heels, off they were; and after darting about after them for a long time, and nearly, once or twice, falling over a precipice, I managed to get hold of the halters; but my fingers were too benumbed for me to hold them, so I handed them over to my friend, who had been enjoying my capers after the ponies, but could not help me, having charge of three camels.

Taking charge of three camels, with a huge whip in my hand, which I could hardly feel, we at last, after a good deal of persuasion, began a move downwards; the huge ungainly camels stepping and sliding about in an alarming manner, and several times bringing our carts unpleasantly close to a precipice at the side of the track. My fellow-traveller went down hill much faster than he wished, as the ponies, setting off, took him down after them at no end of a pace. I found it no easy work to keep on my legs, the snow being excessively slippery, and I expected every minute to have the animals I was leading striding over me. It took us fully half an hour to accomplish this descent; as, so soon as our carts and camels made a helpless slide towards the precipice, they had to be pulled up by turning half round. This sort of operation, in a gale of wind, was very trying; and when at last we did reach the bottom safely our Lama returned thanks to the spirits who, in his belief, had befriended us. We now passed a well which we could never have discovered ourselves. It is curious how the Mongols always know where water is to be found; there are certain indications of its whereabouts perfectly unknown to the stranger. We seldom found them at fault, when a spring was anywhere near, although it often turned out to produce bad and dirty water. Still, we were always too thankful to get any supplies to be fastidious. Monkey now rode away with the water-buckets slung on his camel, to fill them, so I was left to lead the whole caravan, my friend having charge of the ponies. We could not help remarking, what would our friends at home say if they could only see us so employed; dressed in long sheepskin coats, fur boots and large fur hats, with huge whips, trudging along leading a lot of camels on? Of course, no sooner did we find ourselves alone than the camels came loose, and no sooner did we get the one who had come loose attached again than another came undone, and so on until we nearly went mad running about catching them, and all to no purpose. So at last, loosing all patience, I firmly attached the last animal to the one before, as he would come undone every time I started; this answered for a few minutes very well, but the refractory animal suddenly sat down, and as his nose-string was firmly attached to the caravan, it tugged the bit of wood which went through his nostril clean out, and we thought his nose was broken, as it was bleeding; if so, we might as well leave him, as he would be useless; however, he carried our tent and saddles, and as we had already lost one, this was rather a sad contemplation. However, as we could not go on now until the Lamas joined us, we sat down quietly and waited. Monkey soon returning, with plenty of water, eased our minds as regards the camel's nose, and soon placed the leading-string through it again; and suddenly Cocoanut appeared with the missing camel and our baggage, very mysteriously, from a yourt which we passed, which made us conclude that he had gone on the night before to see some friends, taking the baggage-camel as an excuse, and so leaving us to do all the work. It was very impudent, but we could do nothing. This was one of the hardest days we had; and we were not sorry when, after crossing a valley, we encamped at the foot of a mountain covered with snow, which partially screened us from the wind. Here we felt we might bid the desert adieu, although the track is sometimes so designated as far as to Kiachta.

I would strongly advise any who wish to travel by this route to do so at the season of the year that we did; for although it is cold, and the winds are disagreeable, still there is no fear of rain and but little of snow. The ground is in better order, being hard and frozen. In the summer, from all we could learn, the rains are very heavy, which makes travelling disagreeable. The caravans all travel in the autumn and winter months. Travellers should take as little baggage as possible, but be well supplied with stores, for it is difficult in the winter season to obtain even mutton, which in other seasons is abundant.

The camels, if only lightly laden, will do more work and get on quicker. A little broken silver or a few Hong Kong coins will be found useful, and a slab or two of brick tea goes a long way. Travel all day until 4 P.M., stop then until 10 P.M. It is, however, always necessary to look after the guides, as if not urged on they would make longer halts.

The journey through the desert affords but little variety or interest, but it opens the mind to quite a new state of affairs, and a perfectly free wandering life, with no hotel bills to pay or taxes to be summoned for, but simply to take up your quarters where you like and do as you like without reference to any one, is not at all disagreeable for a time. In fact, a degree of perfect freedom is experienced which it would be impossible to find whilst travelling through any civilised regions. Of course one must set out with the full idea of roughing it in the extreme and making the best of everything. It is no use complaining and comparing things with what one is used to find in a civilised quarter of the globe, but having determined to settle down to a month's wandering, must make up one's mind to appreciate and enjoy all we see to the utmost.

It is wonderful how a journey like this developes traits in a man's character. Things that he would have considered impossible of accomplishment at home, become quite easy, and are accepted as a matter of fact, and the bump of invention is certainly wonderfully brightened by necessity. I certainly would not care to make this journey again; but I consider that to a traveller who can afford to take his time, and who likes really to see something out of the ordinary hackneyed beaten track, is willing to rough it when necessary, and is prepared for any emergency, this route is a most recommendable one. Of course, if attacked by sickness in all probability it would go hard with the traveller, as he would find little or no sympathy from the natives, and might probably be deserted by his guides, and never be heard of again, as they would take good care not to turn up at the Russian frontier for fear of being suspected of having murdered him.

The Mongols of the Desert, compared with the Chinese, are certainly inferior as regards inventiveness and cunning; but they are immeasurably superior in other respects, being an open, honest, hardy race of men, hospitable and kind. They are splendid horsemen, and if properly drilled and disciplined would make first-rate cavalry. The Emperor of China, although nominally lord of this part of the world, has no more authority over its inhabitants than I have. They possess however one fault, which is generally found amongst savage nations, that is, an overweening curiosity, which at times we found very disagreeable indeed, and this sometimes merged into a begging propensity; I do not believe for actual begging's sake, but an envy to possess something as a relic from us. We often wondered we were not attacked and robbed, considering how easy it might have been done; but whether our revolvers awed them, or whether out of respect for the Lamas, or on account of their own natural honesty, as a matter of fact we were not molested, except by the wandering Caravan Mongols, who are a very inferior race.

We soon noticed as we advanced onwards that all the yourts were fenced towards the north-east with strong wooden fences, about six or seven feet high, the planks being close together and plastered with mud. This is to give protection against the fury of the winds which prevail, especially in this part of Mongolia, during the winter. To-night we had a long chat about our journey thus far, and felt happy to have arrived safely where we were then encamped; at the same time the increasing cold and severity of the weather gave us warning that unless we wished to trifle with our health we had better now make as much expedition as we could to reach Kiachta. Without giving way to any useless anxieties, we certainly both agreed that we could not well stand a continuation of the hardships we had been enduring for many days longer, at all events. We had one great consolation, and that was, that we hoped to reach the

River Toll to-morrow, and after crossing it to strike on Urga, where a Russian consul lives. We certainly had wandered thus far without any definite idea of our whereabouts, but our calculations as to distances proved in the sequel quite correct.

We started on our way again, rather later than usual, at 11.30 P.M. It was a splendid night, but bitterly cold. Providentially the wind had gone down, which was a blessing we were duly thankful for. All went smoothly except the road, which was one of the roughest we had passed over. We were continuing on a gentle descent, until suddenly down came my camel, and away I slid to the end of my cart, nearly doubled up, and for some time nearly suffocated, unable to extricate myself from my wraps and bags which had descended on the top of me. It took nearly an hour before the camel was induced to rise again, and I had to turn out during that time and stand shivering in the cold. However, we managed after some loss of time to get on again. On the morning of the 12th, we found ourselves in a valley surrounded on all sides by rocky mountains, some covered with fir trees, but all clad with snow. It was bitterly cold, the thermometer standing at 8° above zero. The sun rose about 8.30 A.M., and we could then distinguish faint outlines, to our great joy, of the Chinese town of Mai-Mai-Chin, which means "entrance town," the first town or village we had seen for seventeen days. This made us feel that we were really in the right direction, and in a week at longest would end our journey as far as carts and camels were concerned.

The River Toll or Tula, which is a branch of the Lena before it enters the Lake Baikal, crosses the valley, and we looked forward with much anxiety to reaching its banks, as we anticipated delay and difficulty in crossing it, as at times it becomes very much swollen and consequently is difficult to ford, and there is no ferry communication. All the way this river had been a bugbear to us, as we had heard from Russians that sometimes it was impossible to cross, and so we might be delayed some time, which was a prospect anything but agreeable to us.

We noticed that our Lamas seemed anxious, making use of the word *moo*, bad, and then pointing to the river. As we approached, one of them rode forward to reconnoitre. We fully expected to have to ford the river, and it would necessitate our taking all our bedding and other contents out of our carts, for fear of their being spoiled by the water—no joke on a cold day, when fingers were useless, and besides, a great nuisance, as we should have had to disarrange everything.

Our Lama ahead had reached the river and commenced gesticulating violently; but what he meant until we came up to him we had no idea. When we did so, to our great delight we found that the water was frozen hard; and so now, beyond the difficulty of urging our camels down the steep banks and preventing our carts from capsizing, we had no obstacles in our way.

After a short contest with the camels and a good deal of trouble with our carts, we found ourselves safe at the other side of the river, and congratulated ourselves on having so successfully surmounted what is, at other seasons, the greatest difficulty of the whole journey.

We had been existing on very small supplies of water for some days, so it may be imagined how glad we were to be able to fill our bottles through the holes in the ice, although our fingers were nearly frost-bitten by so doing; and the draught of the pure river-water was the sweetest we had ever partaken of. We had still to pass over a few small streams before reaching Mai-Mai-Chin, and these we crossed also over the ice. On reaching that town we did not enter it, but skirted along outside, passing near a curious burial-ground, surrounded by a high wooden fence, through which we could distinguish rows of huge coffins above the earth; some waiting for a lucky day to be foretold by the soothsayers before being deposited in the ground, and others for transport to the natal place of the deceased; the Chinese being, as a rule, very anxious to be buried with their ancestors, and the survivors of the deceased will pay large sums of money for the purpose, as they fear being otherwise haunted by the spirit of the departed.

Monkey, as usual, here mysteriously disappeared, and we had some difficulty in inducing Cocoanut to take us to the Russian consulate, which is situated between the two towns of Mai-Mai-Chin and Urga, and we could just discern the building in the distance. It was evident that they had made some arrangements, which we however determined to upset, as we had looked forward so long to seeing some human being we could converse with, and perhaps hear some news from Europe At Pekin we had been told that the Emperor Napoleon was dead, and although we did not for a moment credit such an oft-repeated *canard*, still we were anxious to hear if there was any truth in it. So, disregarding the expostulations of Cocoanut, who pointed to the mountain pass on the route to Kiachta, we insisted on that unhappy Mongol's submitting for once to be guided by us.

As we approached, we found the Russian consulate consisted of a group of fine buildings. Entering the yard, we were accosted by a ferocious-looking Cossack, whose language, however, we were unable to comprehend, which seemed rather to astonish that individual. However, we managed, through our usual method of talking, viz., by signs, to get him to conduct us to the quarters of the vice-consul, who received us with the greatest kindness, and was as much pleased to see us as we were to see him, as it was some time since he had seen an European face. He told us he had not been outside the house for three months, and when we expressed surprise, he said, "I have been here five years. I have not a single being except my Cossacks to converse with. I know every inch of the ground, and have no heart to move out." He actually did not know, until we told him, that the river Toll was frozen over, although it was but a short distance from his house. We could not help sympathising with him, as we could imagine what a life it must be, having to stay in such a place.

The Russian government keeps up this consulate at some expense to further Russian influence, which is daily on the increase in Mongolia. There is no doubt but that the frontier will be, sooner or later, advanced to Urga, and the Mongol mind is being prepared for it. The actual Desert of Mongolia finishes here, and Siberia may be said to commence, as the whole features of the country change. The sandy flat plains give way to lofty mountains covered with pine forests, and increasing signs of cultivation. Russian influence, there can be little doubt to the observing mind, will gradually absorb the whole of Mongolia, and probably, in time, China also, and it will be a very good thing too.

The consulate, as I have before said, is situated between the two towns, and so protects all the Russian commerce which passes this route. Mai-Mai-Chin, the Chinese town, is built, with the usual cunning of Celestials, in front of the Mongol town of Kurin, and close to the route which the caravans follow to Kiachta ; and thus all the trade that would go to Kurin is absorbed by it. And a very flourishing trade it must be, as the whole arrangements for transporting goods to and from the desert are made there. Kurin (or Urga, in Russian,) is situated at the end of the valley, surrounded on both east and west by lofty mountains, the western being spurs of the Altais, and called by the Mongols the Holy Mountains, on which no trees are allowed to be felled or game shot under penalty of death.

A Chinese mandarin governor, also a Mongol chieftain governor, resides here; each to protect the interest of his countrymen, as, although the Mongol capital town, it is under the rule of China. But it is the residence of a far greater man, in the estimation of Mongols, than the Emperor of China, viz., the Lama king, who is worshipped by them as a species of deity; and whose infallibility, like that of the Pope, is not at all a subject of dispute. It is estimated that two-thirds of the male inhabitants of Mongolia are Lamas, who would fight at the bidding of their king, who is consequently very much distrusted at Pekin. The Lama king is supposed to have existed since the commencement of the world; on which subject, however, Mongol traditions are very vague. He is supposed never to die, but simply to quit the world, assuming death, and leaving his spirit behind him, which is inherited by another Lama, and so the original king is supposed to live on for ever. But about two years ago the Lama king migrated, and up to the present time no one has been found worthy enough to become the tabernacle of his spirit.

The Mongol population is divided into clans, each of which has its head or chieftain and various petty chiefs. Once every three years, representatives, chosen from each clan, assemble at Urga and compete for prizes; a distinction which, if gained, is held for a year by the clan represented. The sports held are wrestling, throwing the spear, and riding; in which latter accomplishment all Mongols, who are trained to ride from earliest infancy, excel. Few of the Mongols, even of their Lamas, know how to read or write. Their language is distinct from Tartar or Chinese. As they have no literature they adopt that of the latter country. The Lama king is, however, about the only individual in Mongolia who possesses any collection of books, and they are all Bhuddist works.

The Mongols, living as they do in the desert, travelling here and there as the fancy takes them, with their flocks and herds, feel no desire to read, write, or send letters. It seems a pity that the march of civilisation, with its accompanying vices, should ever disturb these harmless simple children of the desert; but come it will. Russia is a powerful and silently encroaching neighbour to have, and China must well know this.

The elevation of Urga is 3500 feet over the sea level.

The whole valley looked dreary and cold at the time we were there. Possibly, in summer it would look better; but, as a residence, it must be most undesirable. We found that the Russian government kept up here, as a body-guard to the consul, a troop of twenty Cossacks.

The vice-consul looked upon us as a godsend, and I am sure we must have done ample justice to the good cheer he set before us, having so long lived on very scanty supplies. The breakfast and dinner he gave us soon disappeared. I felt as if I never could finish eating, and my travelling companion was obliged to remonstrate with me when I came to my tenth tumbler of tea, fearing I should share the fate of the girl in 'Pickwick,' predicted by Sam Weller. We asked for news, but found, beyond the report of the Emperor's demise, nothing new had reached this place. The consul spoke French, and a little English. He wanted us to remain two or three days, and seemed very much grieved when we told him our intention was to proceed onwards that evening, as we dared not now delay longer than possible in Mongolia, as every day the weather was increasing in severity. I am afraid he was half annoyed with us, and thought we did not sufficiently sympathise with his lonely condition.

I must confess that the temptation of passing one night under shelter and getting a good night's rest was very great; and had we not been in a hurry to get to some civilised town, where we could end altogether with the discomforts of an open air existence in an arctic temperature, we should at all events have remained that time.

It seemed quite novel to us, eating in a room, with a table-cloth on the table, after our long roughing in the desert. The rooms were so heated with an enormous stove, whilst all the double windows were hermetically sealed, that, after being accustomed to live out in the open air, the atmosphere was overpowering, and to prevent being suffocated we had to invent excuses to see after our camels every now and then, so as to get a little fresh air. We could easily account for the bad health the consul complained of. To be stewed up in a room where the fresh air never penetrated and to be deprived of taking exercise seemed to us, after our experience, sufficient to cause sudden death.

The vice-consul told us that our trip was the quickest ever made with camels.

He has to get all his supplies of provisions, with the exception of mutton, from Kiachta. We sold our ponies here, and felt a burden off our minds at being quit of them, as we could not help feeling for the poor animals, which were daily getting thinner, and suffering from want of water and too much exercise. And they were keeping us back, as at times they declined to advance, and gave our Lamas no end of trouble.

As before mentioned, our head Lama, Monkey, left us when reaching Mai-Mai-Chin. We did not then know whether we should be able to find the Russian consulate, so said nothing to him, supposing he would know that of course we should, if possible, visit it. During our stay, Monkey, who had seen his various friends and acquaintances, pursued us, as he thought, on the road to Kiachta, and only turned up at the consulate, having retraced his steps, at 7 P.M., looking very tired and disgusted; but we were rather glad, as it served him right for leaving us so abruptly.

This accounted for the state of mind Cocoanut had been in all day, as whenever I went out to see him I found him sitting down in the yard in the middle of the camels. He would get up and point to the hills, saying, "Monkey." We could not at all make out what he meant, so at last he resigned himself to his fate and slept comfortably for the remainder of the time, making one of the camels his pillow.

At 8 P.M., it being a clear moonlight night, we bade our kind Russian host adieu, and left him again to his unenviable solitude, to be broken at some future period by the next traveller who might pass that way; a bad lookout for him, I am afraid.

After leaving the Russian consulate we proceeded a short distance down the valley, in the same direction we had come from in the morning, for about a mile, and then struck into a narrow mountain path on the eastern side of the valley. The cold was intense ; so in order to avoid being frozen we had to walk at a brisk pace, which was a matter of some inconvenience to me, as I was suffering from a blister, brought on by the very rough walking we had been performing during the last few days.

To our great disgust, when we had proceeded but a short distance in the ascent of the pass, our Mongols, who had fasted all day, just like their stupidity, halted at 10 P.M. to get their food. Remonstrance, as usual, was of no avail; so we were done out of a night's travel, for which reason alone we had declined the consul's invitation to remain, and we might, after all, have accepted the shelter he offered us, instead of having to remain in the carts, which were becoming hateful to us, and being nearly frozen hard therein. The moon was shining brightly, and in the pure cold air the whole surrounding scene was perfectly distinct to us. As we stood on the brink of the ascent we had made, some four thousand feet over the sea level, looking down into the valley, we could discover the two towns and the lofty Altais on the opposite side. The river Toll, now hard frozen, looked like a mirror as the moon's beams fell upon it. In front, we looked upon a succession of lofty mountains, covered with pine trees all laden with frozen snow, which in the moonlight gave the branches the appearance of solid crystal. There was no wind blowing, and the deep silence was only broken by the distant howl of the wolf. We would have thought that no living creatures resided in the towns at our feet, so dead and silent were they.

I could not help thinking of the so-called City of the Dead, outside the walls of Canton. But our contemplations and reveries were but of short duration, as, with the thermometer standing at 62° of frost, we had to decide between indulging in sentimentality or being frozen. So my friend, who looked upon my burst of enthusiasm as very appropriate, nevertheless practically suggested adjourning into my cart, where we managed, by a good deal of skill, to sit, one at each end, and so, well wrapped up, commenced a chat over the usual pipe. We were lucky that our tobacco lasted so well; wine and spirits, alas! had disappeared, and of course the longing for a little hot whisky-and-water was the greater now we had none. Here, indeed, I would pathetically warn every traveller to be always well provided with strong liquors, if only to be taken as the venerable Mrs. Gamp took them.

But of course after having, with an infinite amount of trouble, settled ourselves, that is, having arranged our legs so as to avoid reposing our feet in each other's faces, and wrapped ourselves well up, my infernal two-wheeled cart, which was supported in an upright position by a pole from the shaft, commenced a downward descent on its own account, which, as we could not move, was rather exciting, not knowing whether we were going over the precipice or not. But it was soon brought up by the support giving way, and pitching forward, sticking the shafts violently in the ground; the impetus sending my friend's head through the window, which was blocked up with felt, and my toes into the centre of his chest. The lamp was extinguished, and neither of us could move; and it was only after vast efforts, brought on by the desire to avoid suffocation, that I managed to force the door open, tumble out, and then extricate my friend. Our tempers, which were bad at the moment, were not improved by seeing our two Lamas coolly standing inside their tent, roaring with laughter; but a heavy log of wood, which knocked Cocoanut down and nearly sent him into the fire, stopped their mirth, and induced them to assist us in getting the cart in position again. It now being 12 o'clock we determined to make a move, and intimated the same to our Lamas, and, taking the law into our own hands, commenced striking the tent. So after a little grumbling, and a few signs from Cocoanut, whose night it was to sleep, intimating his desire for that blessing of nature, which (as he had been enjoying it more or less all day) we peremptorily declined acceding to, we again commenced our march to Kiachta. But somehow or other we seemed destined to encounter obstacles that night, as we had not proceeded far when down came my camel with a sudden flop, and I, for the second time, was sent like a bundle to the end of my cart. It took us no end of a time to get the camel on his legs again ; I suppose that animal merely preferring to stay where he was to tugging my cart up a steep ascent, which he was nearly unable to do. About 3 A.M., it being the 13th of November, we commenced the ascent of a high mountain pass. I should very much like to be able to give the name of this pass, but it unfortunately has none. Here we found that, after all, Monkey's expedition after us, as he thought, had resulted in some good, as that usually improvident and dense Mongol had actually, to our real astonishment, had the forethought to order oxen, to draw our carts over the pass, instead of our having, as we fully expected, to wait while they were being procured.

Three small strong-looking oxen having been harnessed in the place of the camel into my machine and two into my friend's, which was a light one, away we went straight up a plain of snow. Our drivers were women, clad in skins, and very peculiar they looked, striding away over the snow, whilst we sat in our carts.

Before we started my female driver opened my door and said something to me, but what it meant I do not know, unless, as I suspect, she wanted me to get out and walk, which, however, I did not feel inclined to do, on account of my foot being very bad, for upon looking up the ascent we were going I did not care about trying it, as it seemed like a nearly perpendicular plain of snow, so I preferred to trust to the oxen. I must say, when we had gone half way, and the animals were struggling up and then came to a sudden stop, I could not help wondering, if the cart should commence a retrograde movement, whatever would become of its contents.

After a good deal of exertion and shouting—I think, from the emphasis used, it must have been swearing—we reached the summit, about five thousand feet over the sea level, and looking down we could see that to reach the valley below we had to descend a similar snow plain, which really did look rather dangerous. Here our Lamas intimated that we were to walk; but I could not, on account of my foot, and besides, we had managed to get somewhat warm, and did not feel inclined to turn out; so we flatly refused, which caused our Lamas to indicate, by violently shouting and by signs, that they considered us most unreasonable. At last away we went, and I must say that I was precious glad when, after half an hour's slipping and sliding, and fetching up, by turning the cart half round, at each of which operations it nearly capsized, we reached the valley safe and sound and resumed our way with the camels.

What our Lamas paid for the use of the oxen we could not find out, as that was all arranged in our bargain at Kalgan; but I believe a small quantity of brick tea was all. A lesson drivers of all nations might profit by was, that our female coachmen neither asked us for nor expected drink money.

Proceeding onwards through the valley and still descending, we found ourselves at 8 A.M. of the 13th entering a narrow defile, which brought us into a long valley, and we continued until 1 P.M. to pass through a series of them, with lofty pine-clad mountains on each side, covered with snow. We found here great difficulty in breathing, which of course was attributable to the rarefied atmosphere. We commenced shortly after one o'clock ascending again, and as oxen were not procurable our Lamas, who generally objected to walking, had to dismount from their animals and harness them to our carts, as the ascent was very steep, and it was as much as the combined efforts of the camels could do to draw our carts up. In the afternoon the weather became most delightful, a hot sun and no wind quite warmed us, although it was still freezing hard. We continued to cross a series of small passes very similar to those already traversed; the summit being a round table-land and on each side a valley, surrounded by fantastic-shaped mountains. At four o'clock we encamped in a valley, sheltered from the wind, which was again commencing.

After dinner, at about seven o'clock—the thermometer was then standing at 12° below zero—I was standing at the entrance to the tent, and could plainly discover in the moonlight small frozen crystals dropping, as I looked towards the moon. It was a beautiful sight; it looked like a shower of fire, each little crystal being illuminated as the moon shone on it. This lasted about an hour, the drops being of course frozen dew. Each breath froze; standing in the open air for a few moments was sufficient to cover our beards and moustaches with ice. The elevation we were encamped on was 3900 feet. Our direction was north by a little west. This was our third Sunday in the wilderness; and looking back to the past, to the hardships and difficulties we had passed through, and to our immunity from sickness and danger, we could not help feeling thankful that the journey up to that period had been both speedy and pleasant. In this part of the globe, during the winter months, the sun rises about 30°, so that we never saw it overhead.

The morning of the 14th, as usual, was bright and clear, although intensely cold. Having substituted one of the baggage camels for my usual one I managed to pass a quiet night, as it had not the same habit of suddenly sitting down. It was so cold in the morning that our blankets and coverings were all frozen—I suppose our breath had got upon them; so we were not sorry to walk all day. The country continues to improve in appearance, every sign of the desert being left behind. We could imagine that in the summer it would be very beautiful, as, besides the long grassy plains we passed over, all the surrounding hills were densely wooded, and there were traces of streams and rivulets, then dried up or frozen. The valleys were very fine, and probably in summer would be more thickly populated than they were when we passed through.

More signs of cultivation became apparent; stacks of straw, pens full of sheep, well thatched over; but no traces apparent of the ground being tilled. The natives were much inferior in physique and manners to those who dwell in the desert. They looked more dirty, and seemed poorer, and certainly lack the politeness and hospitality we experienced from their brethren in the desert. It is a curious fact, but it is always the case, that the nearer civilisation or great towns are approached so in like rate does the peasantry degenerate. It was seldom in the desert that we thought our revolvers a protection, but here, I am sure, they were a necessity, and should be shown and kept handy, as some of the peasantry are a sort of half-bred Chinese, and look very villainous and equal to any atrocity. Before encamping, we had passed over a series of passes. At the summit of each we found an obon.

I remember on one occasion we were in advance

of our caravan, and took our seats on an obon at the summit of a pass, waiting for it to catch us up. Being at that time perfectly ignorant as to what it was, we looked upon it only as a curious heap of stones, without thinking how it got there. We commenced throwing the larger stones down the hill. Our Lamas caught us at this act of ignorant desecration on our part, and I shall never forget their looks of horror. I think if they had been able they would have killed us, so angry and horrified were they, and we could not then understand why. It was a long time before they commenced the descent, and then not until their unfortunate camels were nearly plucked bare of hair which they had pulled out, as offerings. If anything had happened on the way down of course it would have been ascribed to our act.

The cold daily increased, and where there was no snow we seldom found water. There is another route, which avoids the steep hills we had to pass over, and water is said to be plentiful there; but it is three or four days longer. We preferred travelling on small allowances of food and water to prolonging our journey, which had become excessively tedious. We were out of the beat of Mongol villages, which, however, was no loss. We saw but very few yourts; it was a blessing when we camped at night to be alone, as the novelty of being mobbed by a crowd of unwashed natives had entirely worn off and we felt inclined to be rude and inhospitable. The nearer we approached Kiachta, when we met with any natives, the more we were liable to be pestered for spirits and gunpowder, so whenever we saw a yourt, instead of riding up to it, as we did in the desert, we went out of our way to avoid it, and took also good care to show no valuables. Money or silver is very much coveted by the natives in these parts, whilst it was uncared for in the desert.

The scenery is magnificent, and if the journey had not been so long and rough we should have appreciated it more than we did; but our failing stock of provisions and want of water or liquid of any kind made us hurry on to reach our destination. I am sure we pictured Kiachta as a sort of paradise, to be reached after much trouble, and looked forward to it as a haven of rest. We found out afterwards that with good ponies we could have ridden the whole way from Urga to Kiachta in two days and nights. The Russian post travels in that manner; and on the way we were passed by a courier, who accosted us in Russian, and seemed mightily astonished that we could not understand him, wondering what sort of people we were; and I fully believe that he led our Lamas to look upon us with suspicion.

CHAPTER VI.

We cross the Rivers Boro and Cara—My Cart sticks in the latter Stream—We ascend the Pass of Cara—The Hills covered with Pine Forests — Delightful Sensation of passing through these Forests after the flat Plain—Oxen procured to make the Ascent—The Top of the Pass marked by a huge Obon made of Wood and Camel's hair—We descend into another Valley—A strange Herd of Cattle—We meet Tartars on Horseback — Their Method of capturing Ponies with the Lasso—A magnificent Prospect—My Health benefited by my open-air Life notwithstanding Privations—The Country becomes more populous as we proceed—We cross the River Sha-Ragol—The Cold increases and the Camels begin to fail – Cocoanut in his Sleep nearly brings the Caravan to grief—We enter a Pine Forest—We reach a vast Plain, at the End of which appear the Spires of Kiachta.

On the evening of the 15th, we crossed a small frozen stream, called by the natives the Boro, and a few hours afterwards we forded the small river Cara. The ice was broken, the stream running very swiftly, but still there was ice enough to enable our carts to pass in two feet of water. All went well, the usual amount of shouting and yelling keeping the camels going until we reached the opposite bank, which was rather steep, when of course my cart, which had been a nuisance the whole way, being much too heavy, stuck, and began to reel over, and all the efforts of the camel, which cried like a child, were unavailing to extricate it. I was comfortably wrapped up inside, but as the cart gradually seemed to be going over I had to jump out, minus my boots and coat, the thermometer standing at several degrees below zero, and aid the Lamas at the wheels. After some time, by the continued efforts of two camels, myself, and the Mongols, it was safely landed, but not without causing me much anxiety, as it sank gradually deeper in the water, and I fully expected every moment to see it turn right over, in which case I should have had my bedding and all I possessed soaked — no joke, when there are no means of drying or of getting others. When we started again I got into the cart, but as the water had touched the bottom it felt like an ice-house, everything inside feeling terribly cold, so my night's rest was done for, and not caring about sharing the fate of the contents of the cart, I dressed and had to walk all night, by which means I just managed to avoid being frozen, for it was bitterly cold. The sun rose at 8.30 A.M., and a beautiful morning it was, and not quite so cold, the thermometer marking 8°.

We were at the foot of the steep and rapid ascent called the Pass of Cara, and as the various tints of the morning sun caught the tops of the hills, and shone on the dense pine forest with which they were covered, making the branches laden with snow of all colors, it was a grand sight. I believe these woods are supposed to contain both wolves and bears, and I should say it was probable, but we saw none. Our Lamas, pointing to my rifle, intimated to us by signs, which we now understood as well as if carrying on a verbal conversation, to have that weapon handy, so for some time I carried it; but finding we had quite enough to do to ascend the slippery pass I soon deposited it again inside my cart. The camels of course were here of no use, so after a short delay we procured five oxen, three for my cart and two for my friend's. The pure bracing air and the glorious scenery we were passing through took away all the fatigue of the night before, and it was really delightful to us, for the first time for so many days, to find ourselves going through those splendid forests which we had only seen at a distance. It was like meeting old friends again, after the desolation of the desert, and had it not been that we feared being frozen to the trees I believe we should have embraced them.

The track we passed over consisted of rocks and stones, covered with frozen snow, which made them so slippery that it was with difficulty we could get any footing at all, and were consequently continually coming to grief. It was a good thing I had given up my rifle. It was a curious sight to see the oxen toiling and struggling up the narrow track, bumping the cart against trees and over rocks; and it was a curious sight to see the contents of these carts after it was all over. Several times we thought we never should get them to the summit, and it certainly was a wonderful thing how our female drivers managed to get the oxen on. Poor Cocoanut, who never would walk when he could ride, came to great grief half-way up, for in his usual manner, when left to himself, he dozed away on his camel's back. The unfortunate animal was sliding about, finding it as difficult as we did to get a footing, when, coming rather sharply against a tree, he sent the sleeping Cocoanut off, who had a tremendous fall, pitching on the top of his head. Luckily his skull was a very tough one; any ordinary one must have been broken. It was impossible for us to avoid roaring with laughter, it was so sudden and such a wakener for him. With many a rueful rub of the head he joined in the laugh. I don't believe it hurt him much. Our progress being very slow we walked on ahead, and reached the summit of the pass. Having the usual table-like appearance, it reached about 5000 feet over the sea level, and 1700 above the plain we had come from. We found a huge obon entirely made of bits of wood and camel's hair, without any stones at all.

As we had to wait for some time we gathered together all the old twigs we could find, breaking a few branches off the nearest trees, and lit up a large bonfire, which kept us warm until the caravan arrived. The view at the summit is closed in by the trees, but as soon as we commenced the descent it broke upon us. We could see a long winding valley running between two mountain ranges, occasionally widening out into a plain. It seemed interminable, especially as we had to go through it. We had evidently crossed the lowest portion of a range of mountains, extending away north and south, and probably the only part where any track exists. The descent into the valley below, which is situated at a greater height than the plain we had left, was soon accomplished, as the course we had to pursue was really straight down, and just short of being perpendicular; so *nolens volens*, carts, oxen, camels, and ourselves, walked, ran, slipped and fell, but without any accident, reached a group of yourts at the foot of the descent; the time occupied being altogether three hours.

There for the first time for some days we got some capital milk, which we boiled with chocolate, and felt quite happy again. If it is not out of place, I would strongly advise every traveller to carry with him a few tins of preserved chocolate with milk and sugar; I do not know what we should have done without it. Even where only the coldest water is to be got it mixes with it, and many a time it formed the only sustenance we got for twelve or eighteen hours.

As we were going to start again my cart was found to be in a rather shaky condition; in fact, looked very much like going to pieces. So we had to tie it up with ropes and substitute a new axle which we carried with us; a labour of some difficulty and time, but still preferable to having to abandon my only shelter at night.

We noticed some very fine oxen, of a very curious breed. They were small in appearance, very strong and well made, with a long fringe of hair on both sides, hanging down below the knees. We only saw them in that valley, and never before or afterwards, so that they must be peculiar to that spot. We passed plenty of sheep and large flocks of ponies, mostly in a wild condition. As we got down the valley yourts became more plentiful, but poor in appearance, although there were signs of a little cultivation, and plenty of vegetation; but the people became more degenerate. Then we came across lots of Tartars on horseback, who would ride up to us and inspect us and go off laughing; however, it was of no use for us to resent it, as we should have soon been overpowered. We saw a rather interesting incident in the afternoon, which amused us very much. A Tartar rode after a pony and threw a noose over its head; and although the animal was nearly strangled, it was for a short time very doubtful whether the Tartar would not be lugged out of his saddle. It was only by the wonderful horsemanship that they nearly all are masters of, that he managed to keep his seat, and reduced the pony to a comparatively tame condition. At about 4 P.M., still proceeding down this long winding valley, we passed a high range of mountains on the right—the name I have forgotten —from the other side of which springs a branch of the river Amoor. We could not find a spot to encamp free from snow, so we had to pitch our tent where it was about a foot deep, and consequently very unpleasant to sit on and equally difficult to get up a fire. However, here we had plenty of wood, having now dispensed with the argolots. We halted at 5 P.M., and for the first time for some days managed, by breaking a hole through the ice on a small river by whose borders we had encamped, to get a supply of really pure water, as all the other streams we had passed were either too hard frozen or, if not, their water was undrinkable. We considered our journey now nearly at an end, and although it was miserably cold, and our usual enemy, the wind, blew as hard as possible, we felt quite cheerful.

I could not help thinking—after a rather frugal supper, consisting mostly of a very hard tongue, which we had several times thought of throwing away, and now thanked our stars that we had not done so—that although I should be very glad when the journey to Kiachta was completed, still that I had derived many benefits from it. When I started from Pekin I was in very poor health, having suffered much from the heat of the Chinese climate. But I felt at this moment as strong and healthy as a man could wish to be. After all it was a life of the most perfect freedom; nothing to trouble one's mind about; no money difficulties, no bills to pay; doing as we liked, wandering where we would, nobody to question us, and no etiquette to follow as a standard of good manners. There certainly was, after all, taking hardships and discomforts into consideration, a great charm in such a life for a short period; and having nearly done it, it was something to look back to and remember during the remainder of one's existence.

What I most regret is the impossibility of giving an entire description of the tents, modes of existence of the inhabitants, and country we passed through, and, indeed, that I could never half do justice to the journey—the events and experiences we had gone through, and which turned out so different to what we had imagined. But few have passed through the tract of country, which is almost unknown, and scarcely any account has been given of the habits and customs of the people who inhabit it.

Before starting from China we had read an account of the journey through the desert, and were very much edified by the conversations that the writer had enjoyed with various natives, as he gracefully reclined at the entrance of their yourts; but as we found a good deal of romance in his accounts, and as moreover none of the party could speak Mongol, we did not derive much benefit from his information.

Before retiring to rest, that is, putting out my lamp and wrapping up, and then wedging myself between two leathern bags, on account of there being no room to stretch my legs straight out (although I am not a tall man) I used to get the cramp so awfully that, forgetting the roof of my cart, I would spring up and knock my head severely against the top. It had become rather warmer, and the snow was rapidly covering everything, but thank goodness the wind had died away. It felt really, with the thermometer at 12°, quite hot. As a proof of what the temperature had been all the way since leaving Kalgan, some fresh beef lasted us twenty days, and was then quite good; and although we had been some days without any stimulants the air was so delicious and renovating that we hardly missed them. We had made forty miles during the day.

We started again in good time, a little before 11 A.M., and had some difficulty in getting the Lamas under way. The nearer our destination appeared to be, the more trouble we had to get these obstinate guides on, and they became unpleasant in their behaviour. I think they rather liked to spin the journey out, trusting to our generosity to pay them the first part of the agreement, although we used to endeavour to impress them to the contrary. Turning out early from my cart on the morning of the 16th, I found it was a cloudy morning, but not so cold, the thermometer marking 14°. We soon commenced the ascent of an interminable pass, and as the roads were partly covered with fresh-fallen snow and deep sand it was very difficult to get the carts on at all. Mine, moreover, required two camels, as unfortunately one of the wheels was out of order. I could not help pitying these poor, patient animals, especially one of mine, a pure white one, which had taken me so long and so well; it looked at me as it laboured on so plaintively, as much as to say, "I am doing all I can." I marched at his side with my Lama's whip—one camel leading, and the other on the opposite side,—but I only made pretence to use it; I really could not beat the poor animal. But we began to be very much afraid of the camels' breaking down, and our having to leave our carts and baggage behind; or, worse still, be delayed perhaps several days, as the country here becomes very mountainous. However, at 10 A.M. we got over the pass and reached some yourts, where my wheel had to be repaired, as it was impossible to go on as it was. So we took the opportunity of getting some milk, and were pestered for money, tobacco, in fact anything we had or were supposed to have. We found we were now getting into a more populated part of the country, as we could discover several groups of yourts, which became more plentiful as we proceeded onwards, bearing the appearance of small farms. The dogs were here a great nuisance, every yourt possessing one; and we had to be continually on the alert, as they are savage brutes and do not at all understand persuasion, unless it be physical.

At 3 P.M. a violent snowstorm came on, and with it a bitter north-east wind, which chilled us to the very backbone, although the thermometer only stood at 16°. We never, even in the desert, felt the cold so much as we did that afternoon, although in my cart the thermometer was as high as 20°. I felt regularly miserable; I had to shut the door and block up the window with pillows, &c., which made it quite dark, and so lie down and be tumbled about. We could not breast the storm, as the sleet cut into our faces. Our poor Lamas certainly behaved well under these trying circumstances; Cocoanut singing one eternal ditty, which he regularly chanted every afternoon for about an hour, in which he was generally joined by Monkey. It was a rude barbaric air, and I often fancied was a sort of hymn; but we got so tired of it that whenever they commenced we used to walk ahead so as to get out of hearing. We generally found when these terrible snows fell down that the thermometer would rise a little but that the cold was much greater to feeling. We considered this day's work the hardest we had gone through, and certainly the most disagreeable. The route from Kalgan to Urga, although uninteresting, as far as scenery goes, compared with that from Urga to Kiachta, is much more enjoyable. Probably we felt it to be so because the journey was becoming wearisome; however, we looked forward to reaching Kiachta the next night; but, as the sequel shows, *l'homme propose et Dieu dispose* was a motto very applicable to our case.

We crossed over the River Sha-Ragol, or Yellow River, so called from the colour of its water, at 9 A.M. Of course it was frozen. Our dinner was very limited that evening, as although we fully expected to end our journey next day still we did not like, in case of accident, to finish our stock of provisions, which was reduced to a bone with a small quantity of mutton on it. So not being in a mood to continue starving, and rather greedily thinking of Russian hospitality awaiting us, we decided to rout the Lamas up early, and at 9 A.M., after a tremendous wrangle, we proceeded onwards. I shall never forget the cold. Our guides were very surly, and so we had to look after the camels ourselves, and it was becoming painfully evident that they were getting used up. We placed the baggage on our two camels, and changed two of the baggage camels with them, and so managed to get on better; but it seemed very slow progress to us, who were all impatience to go ahead. Towards morning, we were proceeding over a plain, and Cocoanut, again sleeping on his camel, very nearly brought himself and the whole caravan to grief. Monkey had gone off to see some neighbouring yourt and bestow his blessing for whatever he could get in return in the way of food; and so Cocoanut was left to lead the caravan on. We walked alongside for some time, giving him a shove with a stick whenever he closed his eyes, to waken him up again. It being too cold to loiter, and thinking he had finished his sleep, we walked on. We had not gone very far when, on turning round, we saw

Cocoanut was again fast asleep and the whole caravan was proceeding towards a deep pit, towards which the camels were being tempted by the appearance of some grass. Already it seemed about to be engulfed. Away we bolted, and came up just as the carts were on the point of rolling over, and taking the whole caravan, baggage and all, to the bottom.

When we awoke Cocoanut with a stone on the top of his skull he was nearly dead with fright, and it required some skill to get the leading camel out of the dilemma. We punished him by pelting him with small stones—an infliction he disliked especially; to avoid it he actually dismounted and had to walk, which he hated nearly as much. Leaving the plain, we had a long steep ascent to pass over, and we then entered into a dense pine wood. The trees were splendid specimens of pine; I have never seen finer. The ground was covered with fresh-fallen snow, about a foot deep; we were very glad it was the case, as our journey onwards from Kiachta we hoped to make in sledges.

We continued still in these woods for fifteen miles; each break we eagerly looked ahead, expecting to see some signs of Kiachta; but without success. The wood seemed as if it would never end, but still it was delightful to wander under those lofty trees, with a bright sun shining and entirely sheltered from the wind. We were also gradually descending, so knew that we must soon reach a plain.

That wretched Cocoanut, whose sleeping propensities seemed doomed to annoy us, especially at this stage of our journey, in the afternoon again brought us to a halt, he having allowed his camel, which was attached to my cart, to take one side of a tree and the cart the other, by which blunder the harness was all smashed and one side of the conveyance stove in. How we did anathematise him, and how provokingly he did grin! And we afterwards had good reason to believe that if not done on purposè by him, Monkey, for his own reasons, had left him in charge.

Vainly did we endeavour to infuse some warmth into our frozen fingers. Mine began to cause me some uneasiness, as they were quite white and dead up to the first joint and I could not feel anything with them. At four o'clock we left the woods and reached an extensive plain, which looked about eight or nine miles across. We could see at the distance a range of hills, and, to our intense joy, two white spires, which told us that at last Kiachta was in sight.

Inciting our Lamas to speed, which they, to our indignation, gave no response to, we proceeded in what seemed in our opinion to be a wrong direction, and which proved to be the case. As we now fully expected to sleep in Kiachta that night a little embellishment was naturally considered necessary, so we mounted into our carts to effect it. My looking-glass, which was freezing hard, only gave me the dim reflection of what seemed a very rough and weather-beaten individual. I regret to say our ablutions had been very few and far between, and our raiment, which had endured all kinds of weather, looked anything but inviting. My top-boots, lined with sheepskin, for want of blacking, certainly did look rather bad. The hard part of the undertaking, I mean substituting another coat for the one I had on, I can scarcely describe. As I have before stated, I could never turn in my cart, so I had to sit on my haunches, with my head bent forwards, and so get out of my clothes. Now imagine, good reader, being placed in this position, with one's fingers frost-bitten, not being able to feel a single thing. What a time it did take me to put on my best coat! And now all the labour was thrown away after all. Certainly, after twenty-two days' wandering, and endeavouring as much as I could to make myself decent, the result was anything but satisfactory; but I did at last wriggle into another coat, and on getting out of my cart looked so spruce that my friend hardly knew me. But what a couple of ruffians the civilised world would have called us! To our intense annoyance, we discovered that Monkey had determined we should not reach Kiachta that night, and it was evident by what we could make out that he was considering the necessity of taking us first to our destination, and then having to return again out of the town with the camels and carts to encamp, which trouble he did not care about entailing on himself. Vainly did we expostulate, scold, and shake our heads, saying, *Lang mongo joss* (No money for you). He was obstinate and determined. It was most aggravating, as we were scarcely two miles from the town.

Threats were of no avail; so what does Monkey do? He suddenly declared he had taken the wrong road, which was very evident, when we found a small river stopped our further progress. In order to demonstrate that we could not pass over he made one of the camels stick its leg through a hole in the ice. Although we perfectly saw through this ruse, we were quite helpless; so tents were pitched, and we, in sight of Kiachta, felt awfully savage. However, our friends the Lamas never knew how much they lost by this move. The money we intended giving them for themselves we reduced considerably.

It was some time before we felt even up to cooking our soup, my friend, who always cooked the dinner, for a long time being too angry to undertake that office; and it was only when driven by the pangs of hunger that we did make our last mess; and it was not a bad one, considering the limited quantity of materials.

After dinner we felt more amiable, and inclined to take the merits of our Lamas into consideration *versus* their demerits ; and we agreed unanimously that they had behaved during the first part of the journey remarkably well, but had fallen off very much during the latter portion. They had had hardly any sleep since we started, except what they got when on their camels; so we decided, taking all things into consideration, to fee them well, but not so well as we had intended. This resolution we arrived at more easily by reason of

Monkey's hostile behaviour during the evening and his obstinate refusal to move on.

The cold on the border of this little river was frightful. I am sure, with the exception of the one hole Monkey had found, it was frozen to the bottom. We passed over safely later on. The mercury on my looking-glass was frozen into small beads, and large stalactites hung from the roof of my cart. As I entered my daily journal the thermometer inside my cart stood at 20° below zero, or 52° of frost, and it was as much as I could do to hold the pencil at all in the benumbed state of my fingers. Every now and then my friend would shout out, "How's the thermometer?" and I invariably found it lower. It was a foretaste of Siberia, and we rather expected to be frozen, for all the wraps we then possessed were not enough to keep out the cold. Luckily there was no wind. We could not help thinking how warm we might have been in Kiachta, and it certainly did not tend to diminish our annoyance at the unnecessary delay.

As may be imagined, we felt a great deal too restless and excited to get much sleep that night, and it was also too cold to do so, as it actually created pain by its intensity; so we were very glad when at six o'clock, it still being dark, on the morning of the 18th, we again resumed our journey, which was then so soon to finish. We passed over the small stream without any difficulty and marched on with a bitter wind blowing; our noses and fingers were frozen, and we suffered for a long time afterwards from the effects of that morning's cold. The thermometer indicated 40° below zero, or 72° of frost, and we were not provided with the necessary fur coats to keep out such cold, so it was a wonder we did manage to stand it all. After a roundabout way to avoid recrossing the small stream which winds about through the plain, at eight o'clock we reached the Chinese town, which is situated similarly to that we passed before reaching Urga, and is also called Mai-Mai-Chin. Here we missed that perverse Monkey, and found he had ridden off without consulting us at all, and instructed Cocoanut to wait at the entrance for him. Now this was too bad, as having to stand still even for a short period was dangerous, and that too within a short distance of the Russian town of Kiachta. It seemed as if just at the last part of our journey everything conspired against us to keep us back.

For some time, Cocoanut, who became suddenly

deaf, refused to move, and we could not go alone, as we did not know the way nor did we care to leave our baggage behind. Vainly did we shout out *Jabo!* (Go on!) for all the reply we got from Cocoanut was, pointing to the distance, " Monkey." How we did hate Monkey! At last however it was necessary to take some determined steps, as we were now surrounded by a mob of Mongols and Chinese, who confused us with the questions they asked, we not understanding one word. We mentioned the name of the Russian gentleman to whom we had letters of introduction, but nobody seemed to know or understand what we wanted. At last, losing all patience, we precipitated Cocoanut from his camel, and, taking the leading-string of the caravan, proceeded with it, followed by him, down the principal street of Mai-Mai-Chin. Cocoanut became obstreperous, and we had to threaten him several times with our revolvers — weapons he had a great respect for—before he gave in. We found out afterwards that as he had never been there he was afraid of missing Monkey and being left to his own devices, not knowing where we should go to, or if Monkey would be able to find us out.

We marched along a wide street, passing the

P

Chinese governor's house and a very handsome temple, noticing some very fine-looking shops on our way, and at last emerged from the Chinese town and found ourselves in a sort of neutral piece of ground, beyond which is situated the wooden town of Kiachta, and at the entrance a very handsome church and the residence of the commissaire impériale.

Here we found a few half-civilised looking beings, who informed us where the house was we were bound to. The respectable portion of the community was evidently kept indoors by the cold, and very wisely too.

We soon reached the residence of M. —— and presented our letters of introduction. Our appearance was anything but presentable, but must have been impressive; nevertheless, contrary to our expectations, for we only calculated upon being shown where we could obtain lodgings, we were received with a most hearty welcome; a room was placed at our disposal, and we were told to make ourselves comfortable and at home.

There are no people like the Russians for kindness and hospitality. We had not the slightest claim, neither had we the slightest expectation, of being so heartily received.

It may be imagined how glad we were at last to find ourselves safe and sound under shelter again and in the midst of civilised human beings like ourselves. For a time, while we were unloading our carts and camels, we could not help thinking, as we watched the contents gradually being taken out, how long we had inhabited those uncomfortable conveyances, and through what privations and hardships we had passed; and a feeling akin to wonder came over us that we had been able to do the journey so well and without being visited by sickness.

How long it had seemed when we were at it! And now it was all over and we had the pleasure of finding ourselves safe, the difficulties were nearly forgotten, and it appeared as if only a short time ago we were at Kalgan.

Monkey turned up, of course, when all the work of discharging our cargo was done, but we were in good spirits, so did not scold him as we had intended to do, when we were exposed to the cold. What a quantity of things came out of our carts and was unpacked from our camels! When they were in the room we could hardly turn. We took a farewell look into what had been our only shelter for so long a time, and very very thankful we were to be quit of them for ever.

We had made the journey in one day over our contract time, twenty-four days, but did not insist on the fulfilment of the terms. We presented each Lama with a lump of sycee worth about £1 5s. each lump, which delighted them highly. They little knew that we had intended giving them more had they behaved better during the latter part of the journey. We also presented them with any remnant of stores we had, and our sheep-skin coats, which were of no use, being nearly worn out, and all odds and ends we did not want, and wished them good-bye. Shaking hands with them, which they considered as a sort of a blessing, we bade our unwashed Mongols adieu without much regret.

How delighted we were to get a wash and to change our raiment, and then to sit down before a well-stocked table and eat our fill! The great drawback we agreed was, that our kind host could only speak or understand his own language; but a young lady living with the family appeared later on and acted as interpreter, speaking French.

A few remarks will finish the first part of our

journey, which I have so feebly endeavoured to narrate.

I am sure from what I saw that the autumn and winter seasons are the right ones for travelling across Mongolia. There is no fear of rain, which in summer is abundant and renders travelling difficult. The small rivers we passed over at the latter part of the journey were all frozen, and so did not raise that hindrance to our progress which in other seasons they would have done. Another great reason for preferring the winter months is, that the camels are in good travelling order, which they are not in summer. Of course the hardships from cold and lack of water are great, but still as we were able to endure them others could do so likewise; and after all, cold is preferable to intense heat, as it is possible to keep the body warm through exercise.

I would strongly advise any one who may wish to travel over this route to provide himself with a good light cart, although the having it made may entail a loss of a few days at Kalgan, as it is of the greatest importance to be provided with a shelter as comfortable as possible to last some twenty to thirty days. Mine, which was badly constructed, being much too heavy, and only five feet six inches long and about two feet and a half wide, was an aggravation of misery to me the whole way.

Baggage should be as small as possible. It is not necessary to carry much clothes, a fair supply of flannel shirts, &c., and a few pairs of good thick trousers, a coat or two, and some strong boots and fur gloves, would be enough, as all the necessary outfit for Siberia is to be procured either at Kiachta or Irkoutsk. Plenty of stores and wine, however, is very necessary. We found the preserved chocolate in tins most useful.

For money purposes, six or seven dollars or broken silver and a few bricks of tea are quite sufficient, the rest being in letters of exchange on merchants in Kiachta.

There is not much of interest in this part of the journey, but it opens out the mind and gives the traveller a knowledge of quite a new state of existence. A wandering life, with a sense of perfect freedom, for a limited time, also bears its own reward.

I certainly should not care to make the journey again; but I consider to the already experienced traveller, who wishes to see the world and gather wisdom from so doing, and who is tired of the hackneyed tourist routes of Europe, and is willing to put up with every species of hardship and not afraid to face danger and rough it in the true acceptation of the word, this is a most recommendable journey.

There are three routes marked on my map from Kalgan to Urga: the one usually travelled over by caravans; another, which we came by, rather shorter; and one—the longest—reserved by the Chinese government for post couriers. This latter route skirts the desert, and consequently runs where more vegetation exists. The post service, which is uncertain, is performed by Chinese couriers on ponies—a journey which they make very much at their leisure. Ponies are only obtainable at the outskirts of the desert for this service.

The inhabitants of Mongolia are divided into clans, but as they have no method of obtaining a census their number is unknown.

Few of them, even of their Lamas, know how to read or write. Their language is akin to that spoken by the Tartars and distinct from Chinese; but the character used is Chinese, they having no letters or literature of their own. They live in the desert, and travel about as fancy suits them with their flocks and herds.

It seems a pity that the march of civilisation

with its accompanying vices should disturb the life of these primitive children of the desert, and destroy their simplicity and happy ignorance; but come it will; in fact it is fast intruding under the auspices of Russia—a powerful and silently encroaching neighbour. China must now feel this; that is to say, if any thought ever occupies the minds of the ignorant, barbaric, self-conceited mandarins at the court of Pekin. Russia, with her vast influence, herself hardly yet entirely civilised, stretches out her arms on all sides, and will swallow up China itself in her embrace at some not very far distant period; and it would be a matter of congratulation if the present Chinese government, with its cruelties, ignorance, vice, and hatred of foreigners, were to become a thing of the past and be swept from off the face of the earth.

Mongolia Proper is divided into two great divisions: North and South. The first comprises four provinces, the second eight or ten. Its resources are speculative, as so little is known about the country.

Our journey from Kalgan to Kiachta was considered by natives as one of the quickest ever accomplished with camels, and it also excited some astonishment at the freedom from danger and sickness we had experienced, considering the period of the year.

The next portion of our journey will be perhaps more interesting, but certainly not so novel and strange as that I have endeavoured so imperfectly to relate.

CHAPTER VII.

Kiachta—The Luxury of a Russian Bath after our Travels—We visit the Commissaire Impériale — Method of conducting the Postal Routes—Method of warming a Russian House—Festivals of the Jour de Nom—Curiosities of Costume in Russia—We meet an Englishman—A Russian Dinner—The Ladies' Room—Russia the great Cigarette Country—The Riches of the Kiachta Merchants —The Magnificence of the Greek Church—The Chinese Town of Mai-Mai-Chin adjoining Kiachta—Signs of its Importance and Wealth—The Yamun of the Chinese Governor—We experience the Advent of Civilisation by sending a Telegram to London—An English Dinner at last—A Russian Gentleman agrees to join us in a Tarantass on our Journey to Irkoütsk—Hospitality of the Russians—Their Acquaintance with English Authors—The Bread-throwing Custom—A Description of the Town of Kiachta—Expenses of our Outfit and Postal Blanks for our future Journey— We start in our Tarantass, and arrive at Auskiachta, where our Russian travelling Companion, Col. B——, joins us—We proceed onward to Korai—Tremendous Pace of our Tarantass downhill.

WHAT a delight it was to find ourselves once more amongst people we could converse with in French and German, and find ourselves safely housed and relieved from all anxiety with respect to our dinner, &c.! Luckily the bath-room, with which every Russian house is supplied, was already heated—it takes generally twenty-four hours to get up the

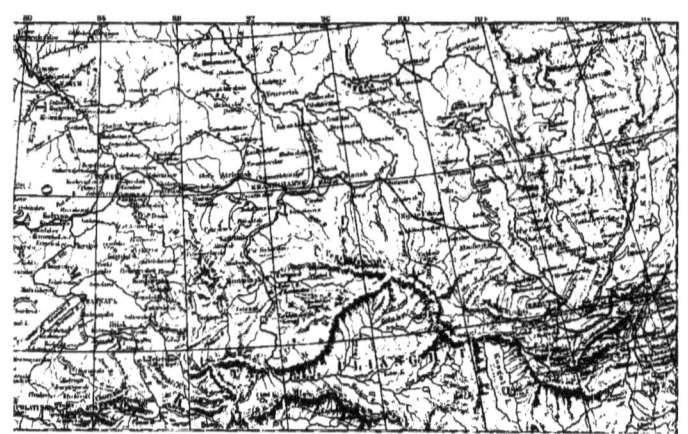

necessary amount of heat—and to this part of the establishment we soon found our way, as it may be imagined, with great delight, for in the desert I am afraid we had nearly forgotten that there was such a custom as washing.

We had to walk across a yard, and we soon experienced the difference between the cold and heat of the bath-room. It was the first time we had ever been into a Russian bath, and the effect upon us, especially upon my friend, was something astonishing and unpleasant at first. But I think the bath deserves a description.

It stood alone in the centre of a yard, in a small wooden building. Preceded by a servant, armed with small rods, which looked like branches with dead leaves, that in the heat gave a fragrance to the building, we entered into an outside room, where we took off our clothes. We then walked into a room which looked like a washing place; having on one side a huge sort of boiler, and steps all round. Our attendant made signs to us to ascend these steps, which we did slowly, as the higher we mounted the hotter it got. Panting, hardly able to breathe, we reclined on the top step, when our attendant commenced throwing water on the outside of the furnace. We saw directly columns of steam coming towards us, which no sooner did we feel than with a yell down the steps we rolled. It was more than we could stand. My friend had to be taken into an ante-room in a fainting condition and I staggered out also. However, after a time a good soaping and washing and scrubbing with cocoa-nut fibre revived us, and we left the bathroom weaker but cleaner, but not at all agreeably impressed with it. Strange, however, we did not feel the cold, which was then most intense; much more so than before.

Having now made ourselves somewhat respectable, and well wrapped up in fur coats, kindly lent to us by our host, we proceeded in a sort of *char à bancs*, drawn by a splendid little horse at a rapid pace, to Mr. Pfaffius, the commissaire impériale, by whom we were most kindly received. We handed him our passports and inquired about procuring the necessary postal blanks to take us to Ekaterinburg, and he gave us all the necessary information. Monsieur Pfaffius first viséd our passports, and we then sent them to the commissaire de police, from whom we then received the postal blanks. For travelling through Siberia as far as Ekaterinburg the whole postal route is under government. The different stations are farmed out to speculators, some taking ten or a dozen, and letting them again to others; but government exercises authority over them, and when not efficiently kept at once withdraws the contracts and relets them to others.

The great thing, if possible, is to procure a pass with two stamps, which however is only given to government couriers; these take precedence of all on the road except what is called the "gold courier," or heralder of the approach of government gold, who, besides having two stamps, has an endorsement to that effect on the pass.

To merchants and ordinary travellers only one stamp is accorded, which is merely a permission to travel, but gives no guarantee of speed, or certainty of obtaining horses. Of course we could only obtain the one stamp, but we relied on being passed on by travelling with Russian officials; a fact which we accomplished. It seemed so strange, bowling away at so many miles an hour—after the tedious motion of the camels—having to hold on at the corners for fear of being whisked out. Everything of course to us was *couleur de rose*.

The gentleman we stayed with possessed all sorts of vehicles, all good and well-made, and also capital steeds. The wealthy portion of the inhabitants mostly drive; we noticed very few walking; of course in summer it may be different. In winter it is even too cold to walk. Sitting down well wrapped up, one's feet enveloped in a sort of huge golosh lined with fur, which every Russian wears and on entering a house leaves in the hall, is warmer than walking. Besides, taking exercise in a huge fur coat down to the heels, is embarrassing. There was one thing we found most trying, after the free-air life of the desert we had led. The houses were all heated up with immense stoves; generally one or two large ones in the centre of the house, by which means a portion is let into the walls of the various rooms. The double windows were also all hermetically sealed. It was truly awful to us, after living so long in the open air; we felt quite stifled, and every now and then had to rush out into the open to get a breath of air. Besides, it must be dangerous, going out from such a temperature. We both felt upset and sick. On entering a house a blast of hot air meets one, and certainly we used to perspire and feel very faint. I think this accounts for the want of colour in the faces of the inhabitants in Russia generally.

It is the fashion in Russia to celebrate what is called the *jour de nom*, and this not being the busy season we found ourselves in for a lot of entertainments, which we forthwith unanimously resolved to enjoy. A *jour de nom* means, if the gentleman or lady of the house is blessed with the name of the particular saint which occurs on any given day, all friends and acquaintances go and congratulate him or her, and remain in a continual state of eating, drinking, and playing cards (which last all Russians are addicted to) from morning until evening.

The day we arrived happened to be one of these festive occasions at the richest merchant's house. Our host, who was going to give his congratulations, took us with him, and there we at once met and were introduced to all the notabilities of Kiachta and Troizkozavsk, which is the town proper, being about two miles from Kiachta, which is merely the mercantile station; whereas at Troizkozavsk all the officials live, with the exception of M. Pfaffius, and the telegraphic communication to St. Petersburg commences there. Received with the greatest cordiality, which was indeed the case all through Russia, we were speedily attracted to a sort of buffet covered with tempting viands and rows of bottles of wine of all kinds. We soon found ourselves drinking the health of the lady of the house, our own, and everybody's; feeling, after such a long abstention from all strong liquors, we really ought to make up a little for it. During the afternoon the ladies—who all sat in one room, and consequently made shy men feel inclined to keep away from that part of the building—formed a pretty picture, most of them being good-looking and lively—entertained themselves, no doubt, with the latest scandal or fashions, and smoked cigarettes. They were all remarkably tastefully and well dressed. The gentlemen sauntered about, played whist, or strummed on the piano—amusements they varied by continual applications to the buffet. A curious custom there and throughout Siberia is, that gentlemen dress in what we call evening clothes in the afternoon, and appear in the evening in frock coats, &c. As of course we were not aware of this fashion we exactly reversed their custom. At about three o'clock, everybody being full of good things, and ourselves especially being nearly dead with heat, we proceeded to make our adieus. The host then invited his particular friends to return to dinner at four o'clock, and we had the honour of being included amongst that number, so we emerged into the open air and were soon refreshed by a rapid drive through the bracing cold at a tremendous pace. Our driver, who was three parts drunk—we afterwards found out that this was the custom amongst *yemschiks*, and particularly with ours—lashed his horse into a gallop, and it required all our skill to enable us to remain seated on the side seats of the trap, a sort of outside jaunting-car. However, as we did not know how to say "slower" we soon began to enjoy the excitement, and were sorry when we spun into the yard of our home. Having changed our apparel, away we went again at railway speed to our dinner party. The first person we met on entering was a countryman of mine, Mr. Grant. We had often heard of the one-legged Englishman, and it may be imagined how delighted we were at last to be able to converse freely with some one besides ourselves, as although anything but weary of each other, we had long ago exhausted our mutual stock of conversation.

Another English gentleman, who assists Mr. Grant in his telegraphic duties, appeared, and I am sure we overwhelmed them with inquiries of all kinds, most good-naturedly answered, too, on their parts. We were now summoned to dinner by our host, whose hand I again solemnly shook for about the fiftieth time that day, and procuring seats next to Mr. Grant we sat down to a well-stocked table, extending all round the room. About one hundred sat down to dinner. A Cossack military band discoursed lively airs during the meal. Alas! my appetite had somewhat faded with the continual application to the buffet I had gone through in the afternoon. Porter, which costs there about three roubles, or nine shillings, a bottle, was handed round in small tumblers, and consumed very largely. It is very strong, being no doubt a peculiar brew made to suit the climate, as I have never tasted its like in England. At the conclusion of the dinner, following the lead of our host, we all rose, and being all supplied with champagne, which in Russia is generally drank after dinner and not during dinner, we drank to the health of the hostess. We then marched round the table towards the ladies' room, where we shook hands with the host and the hostess, everyone saying something, but not knowing Russian we contented ourselves with the shake of the hand. We then again left, being invited to return to the ball at eight. I was now beginning to feel tired. For the first day we had done pretty well, so I took the opportunity of getting a snooze. But how I did wish we could open a window to air our room! We nearly determined, in our desperation, to fall against a window and smash a pane, by mistake.

At eight o'clock we found ourselves at the ball, and there were lots of girls, some good-looking and very rich, but unfortunately few who could speak any other language than their own—Russian. We danced away for some time, being introduced to nearly every one; but what with porter, sweet Russian wine, champagne, &c., and the intense heat of the room, I was glad to steal away quietly at twelve o'clock, and reaching home proceed to sleep. My friend, anxious to keep up our reputation as being able to drink against any Russian, found a hard head in the commissaire of police, and the result was that at 4 A.M. he tumbled over me as I lay on the floor, and woke up later on with a very bad headache, which however we attributed to the bath. So ended our first day in Kiachta.

We did not feel much inclined to rise before ten, after our last day's exertions. We then proceeded to our host's office, and found him busily engaged with Chinese and Mongols. We wished him good morning, and smoked out the usual cigarette. I believe Russians smoke cigarettes all day. The first thing, on entering a room, you are presented with a cigarette—and very good ones as a rule. Wherever we went, we always found the box of cigarettes. Spain is a cigarette country, but I fancy Russia is even more so.

I found in my diary the following remarks, which perhaps may not be out of place here :—

"The merchants in Kiachta are mostly very rich, a great many of them possessing large shares in the gold mines in Eastern Siberia. Formerly, before the northern ports were opened in China, they had the whole monopoly of the tea trade with Russia, but of late years that has diminished, and now, with the Suez Canal open, it will still further decline. They generally live in fine large houses, all built of wood, and capitally furnished. They live well, and seem to swim in champagne and porter. The women are good-looking and most amiable."

On Tuesday, the 19th, we paid a visit to the Greek church, which is a very handsome building indeed; but, although to say so to a Russian would create great offence, we could not help thinking that it looked remarkably like a Roman Catholic church. It was wonderfully decorated with pictures, all of a religious tendency, but not of very great value in an artistic point of view; a great deal of gold and glitter appeared everywhere. Altogether, the orthodox Greek church did not come up to our ideas of simplicity. The whole effect was decidedly gaudy.

We witnessed a service in the minor, or winter, church, which is a small portion set apart for the cold season, heated to a very disagreeable extent. The singing, which was conducted by a choir of seven, was execrable. In Greek churches there are no organs. The priests, who wear long hair, in their dress and manner of worship reminded us much of Rome; and I am afraid we were not as impressed as we wished to have been. A stranger would put Russia in the first category as a candidate for being styled a religious nation, as certainly in every small village one or more fine handsome churches exist; but I think the outside of the platter signifies more than the actuality.

After leaving the church, bent on sightseeing, we paid a visit to the Chinese town of Mai-Mai-Chin, named the same as the town situated in front of Urga.

There were abundant evidences of wealth; the streets, at least the principal one, consisted of certainly the finest Chinese houses I have ever seen, with large courtyards, full of merchandise; and from the interiors of one or two houses we were allowed to see, we concluded the owners must be possessors of great wealth. The Chinese certainly, as far as Kiachta, outwit the Russians and Mongols, as the two towns take a good portion of the trade.

We visited the *yamun* of the Chinese governor: a very handsome edifice, containing a temple for his Excellency's own use. We happened to see his Excellency and suite, who were proceeding to the temple to satisfy their consciences before indulging in the pleasures of the day, and they looked miserably cold. I should think they devoutly wished themselves back again in their own sunny clime. The Chinese are wide-awake enough to recognise Russia as a dangerous neighbour, and so always send a mandarin of high rank as governor to Mai-Mai-Chin—a post I believe, however, not much coveted.

We tasted a very peculiar *samshue* (spirit made from rice) here, not at all like the same spirit in China. It has an aromatic flavour, and when heated, and taken in little cups, is not at all disagreeable.

Having satisfied our curiosity as to Mai-Mai-Chin—there not being much to see—we drove over to Troizkozavsk, and had the pleasure of sending a telegram to London, which made us feel quite civilised again.

We then proceeded to visit various shops, for the purpose of buying skins for the journey to Irkoutsk, and we managed to buy each of us a very good *deehar*, or reindeer skin, which is the best outer coat to be got, as it keeps out the wind and cold. It is a mistake to attempt to purchase the whole outfit for the journey through Siberia at Kiachta; it is much better to get the deehar, some felt socks which pull over the boots, and a pair of fur gloves, and wait until reaching Irkoutsk, where everything is much better and cheaper. Our deehars cost us twelve roubles, equal to £1 16s., and they lasted us well the whole way to Moscow. We finished our day by dining with Mr. Grant, and if the telegraph had inclined us to feel we were getting near home, how much more did the capital English dinner, first-rate beer, and genial conversation of our kind host make us feel even closer still!

I began to feel rather alarmed about my fingers, which, as far as the first joints, had become useless. They were white and dead, and my alarm was not diminished by being told that if they turned black they would fall off. It may be imagined how anxiously I continually looked at them, as hourly they became more useless.

We found that, as far as we were concerned, the fuss made in Pekin, at the British legation, regarding the necessity of having a Chinese passport—to obtain which a delay of a day or two invariably occurs—was unnecessary, as we were not once asked for them; but we had to produce them for our Mongol Lamas. This was doubtless because they had neglected to provide themselves at Kalgan. Redtapeism is the same all over the world, and especially so where an English embassy exists.

We returned home after our dinner, as we had to dress for another dance. We were nearly frozen, as the wind met us. During the evening our kind host, who accompanied us, and always insisted on seeing us well wrapped up in furs, without which we should have been frozen, introduced us to a Colonel B——, a Russian gentleman of great wealth and influence, who intended shortly to depart to Irkoutsk, where he lived. He informed us he had two tarantasses, and most kindly offered us the use of one, and asked us to accompany him. This was exactly what we desired.

We had been very much puzzled about procuring a tarantass, which is the only vehicle used, to make the journey, at least as far as Irkoutsk. It is a sort of long, old-fashioned looking carriage on four wheels, with a hood; the springs are made of wood, and a good thing too, as over the roads it has to go no steel ones would hold out long. It is a comfortable sort of a conveyance, being long enough to lie down in. The great art consists in packing all the luggage at the bottom as flat as possible, filling up all the crevices with straw or hay, and so forming a comfortable bed to recline on. The jolting and shaking about and the rattle this wonderful vehicle produces surpass all description. When I first saw a tarantass it certainly, in idea, took me back at least two centuries, for anything so out of date I had never seen.

This kind offer of Colonel B—— took away all anxiety as to our journey as far as Irkoutsk, as he was travelling with a two-stamp pass, which would insure speed and attention. It is curious that at Kiachta, notwithstanding the intense cold, snow rarely falls, and even if it does, the wind which sweeps across seldom allows it to remain and so form a snow road; thus sledging is nearly unknown there, and seldom commences before reaching Nijni Oudinsk. We had hoped to commence sledging at once, but, anyhow, it is always better, even if there is snow enough, to wait until arriving at Irkoutsk before purchasing a sledge, as the selection, of course, is larger and better.

We may certainly affirm that up to that time we had been most fortunate, both in having crossed the desert so quickly and so well, and then in having fallen amongst so many kind friends, whose chief object seemed to be to insure our comfort, and render us every kindness and assistance in their power. Such kindness I am sure we shall never forget; it made us frequently remark that the Russians were the most hospitable and friendly people we had ever met, and most refined and luxurious in their mode of living—an impression we never lost as long as we were on Russian soil.

It is often stated that the Russians are not yet half civilised; I can only say we found translations of most of our celebrated English authors, and even of our periodicals, at most of the houses, and also that they were well-acquainted with the names and works of our principal English novelists, and with the latest even trivial doings in England. They are very fond of music; at nearly every house we found a splendid piano and somebody who could play well on it.

I am afraid I have diverged from my subject, but the recollection of the many friends we made in Kiachta must be my excuse.

We remained, as usual, late, amusing ourselves with dancing, eating, drinking, smoking cigarettes, and watching the various whist tables. All Russians are passionately fond of cards, and generally play well and for large stakes; their whist is rather different to ours, being very complicated in marking the points. I played a few games at *écarté*, while my friend joined in whist, but our success was not such as to raise our reputation for card-playing.

The rooms crowded, not a bit of ventilation, and a huge stove, sending out volumes of heat, rendered the atmosphere intolerable. I never could make out how they could even breathe in it, but no one beyond ourselves seemed in the least inconvenienced by it. At supper, all sitting down, and being provided with everything very good, we learnt a new custom—I believe, peculiar to Kiachta. When any gentleman fancies a lady— of course he is intimate with her—he throws a small pellet of bread at her; if she takes it kindly he is a lucky man. My neighbour commenced throwing bread at a young lady, the richest belle of Kiachta, and, after each pellet, ducked behind me, so that I was surprised to see her darting angry looks at me. But it was only afterwards, when I asked her to dance and received an indignant refusal, that I learned she had resented what she imagined was my rudeness in throwing pellets at her, being a stranger. Of course I explained my innocence and was immediately acquitted.

At a late hour we returned home, feeling very different to what we used to in the desert. Civilisation had already bestowed her doubtful blessing on us in the shape of a headache next morning.

The town of Kiachta, at first approach, looks very well, especially to those who have come from the barren desert of Gobi. There is nothing like contrast to enhance the merits of the better of the two. The first thing which strikes the eye is certainly the lofty cupola of metal of the handsome Greek church I have before referred to. All the houses in the town are, as before stated, built of wood; and this fact, combined with the dreadful heating apparatus found in them, will account for its having been twice burnt down. It derives its wealth, which is very considerable, from the fact that all goods to and from the desert pass through it to be redistributed elsewhere.

I am afraid I am somewhat repeating myself, but if I reiterate, it is purely for the sake of those who may travel that way.

It is necessary on arrival to visit first the commissaire impériale, to get the Russian passport viséd, and then to send to the commissaire of police to obtain the necessary postal blank, which cost us, for three horses as far as Tumen, fifty-five roubles. Of course this does not include the cost of the posts, the amount being merely for the pass. With the pass for three horses four can always be obtained, only paying for three; and when required, five for four.

Troizkozavsk is the town situated a short distance from Kiachta—about two miles. Troizkozavsk is the aristocratic town, where all the officials, military men, and other swells reside. It is situated north of Kiachta, and is about two miles distant from that mercantile town. There are a fine church there and some very good shops. The aristocracy who reside there rather look down upon the dwellers in Kiachta. The true Russian has a horror of trade, and although perfectly allowing its utility and necessity, despises the merchant who carries it on.

Mai-Mai-Chin, the Chinese town, which means " entrance gate," I have already fully described.

In the evening of the 21st, our last in Kiachta, we visited the circus of M. Soulier, an enterprising Frenchman, who had travelled with his horses, &c., the whole way from Constantinople, and now was making preparations to cross to Pekin. Of course he was very anxious to have all the information we could give him, which we were only too glad to impart, and I must say we did not, by our accounts, much cheer him up. We have not yet heard whether M. Soulier succeeded in crossing the desert, but I should think he must have lost most of his horses on the way. We did not much enjoy the performance, as the cold was awful, and obliged us to leave early for fear of being frozen.

We certainly arrived at Kiachta at the right

time, as it was the gay season. During the winter months there is but little business doing, and the people give themselves up to thorough enjoyment.

We terminated our visit at Kiachta on the 22nd, and I am sure we carried away with us the most lively remembrances of the kindness we received from our kind host and M. Pfaffius and all those we became acquainted with. From Mr. Grant we received every attention and kindness. We had heard much of him before, and found that the character he bore for hospitality, &c., was not exaggerated. Arriving, as we did, as perfect strangers, all the kindness we received was most generous, and the assistance we got on all sides was most unexpected.

At 12 M. on the 22nd of November we bade adieu to our kind host and his family, and having with some difficulty stowed ourselves away in our tarantass, which, in the way it was then packed, certainly did not impress us with the idea of comfortable travelling, for several days and nights, we rattled away, jolting about sadly, towards Troizkozavsk, to the residence of Mr. Grant, intending there to take our final meal, and halt for Colonel B—— to join us. As it may be useful to future travellers, our expenses at Kiachta were as follows:

	Roubles.
Postal blank	55
One large deer-skin coat	12
3 pairs gloves, lined with fur	5
Felt stockings, 2 pairs—very useful indeed, to pull over boots	3
An Astracan hat	6
	81

My expenses, beyond those before stated, across Mongolia amounted to—

	Taels.
One pony	10
Milk, meat, &c.	5
Present to Lamas	5
	20

The weather had moderated, and it was much warmer, as we drove along; and being wrapped up in our skins, and wedged into a compound of mattresses and luggage, we were nearly stifled.

When we arrived at Mr. Grant's the first operation was to repack our tarantass. We discarded one of our mattresses and several of our packages, and managed to arrange a tolerably comfortable bed upon which we could lie down at full length. The worst of it was, that when we were on the way we immediately got jolted down towards the end of the vehicle, and it was no easy matter, cumbered as we were with clothes, to manage to raise ourselves up again. For those who have been accustomed to travel comfortably by railway, the discomforts attendant upon riding in a tarantass would be nearly unbearable; but to us, after the miseries of the desert, of course any mode of conveyance approaching to speed was a luxury and refinement of travelling. I have often afterwards thought of our rattling old trap, jumping and jolting along, each motion enough to break one's bones. I did once put my head against the side of the hood, and the concussion it received nearly dislocated my neck.

It was 9.30 P.M. before we left Troizkozavsk, as our friend Colonel B—— did not turn up, and even then only sent us a message telling us to go on to the first station and wait for him there. So at last, with many farewells and rather dismal ideas of the length of the journey before us, in a Siberian winter, away we went.

How heartily did we wish we were nearer St. Petersburg! After a smart drive, not being yet accustomed to the noisy movements of our tarantass, we arrived at the first station, Auskiachta, at 12 P.M., rather bruised and sore, the distance from Kiachta being twenty-two versts.

R

We found there a clean room, but of course heated up to suffocation. Unforeseen difficulties now arose, as our friend Colonel B—— had not arrived, and the postmaster asked us some questions which, as we did not understand one word, we could not answer, which certainly did not increase that worthy official's respect for us. We had written down several phrases, and we now began to consult our list of them and hazarded a few as a trial, but with no result. I suppose our pronunciation was wrong, or we had written them down wrong. We said, however, *Loschide getovar*, which means "Get horses ready at once," and this was going to be carried out, which rendered us nearly frantic, as we endeavoured to explain that we must wait for Colonel B——. I think we had written another sentence, and had spoken it by mistake. However, we mustered up courage, after our miserable failures, to say, *Samovar*, and with its assistance we soon made some tea, which we always carried with us.

We began to get seriously uncomfortable as hour after hour passed, and our anxieties were only relieved at last by Colonel B——'s appearance at 4 A.M. He had left after us, through some misunderstanding, which caused the delay.

We fully recognised the fact that in a country like Siberia, having a postal blank with only one stamp, and no knowledge of Russian, it would be no easy matter to travel as strangers, alone; and we felt proportionately thankful that we were so lucky as to have found a travelling companion.

Horses being soon placed into our tarantass, we deposited a small coin, 20 kopecks (100 in a rouble), on the table, for the use of the samovar, re-entered our tarantass, and slept away until we arrived at Korai, at 8.30 A.M. on the 23rd, having done twenty-five versts from last station. The route was hilly and sandy. It is of very rare occurrence that snow ever falls in these districts. Here we breakfasted, swallowing several tumblers of hot tea, which we found most refreshing. It is always necessary to take a sufficient stock of provisions, as eatables are rarely obtainable at the post stations. It is the custom to give the driver a small *navodka*, or drink money, according to the speed he has driven at. In sledges, by promising 40 kopecks, we sometimes attained the speed of 16 miles per hour; but the usual drink-money is 20 kopecks. As an example of the cost of posting, our three horses, from Auskiachta to Korai, cost 1 rouble, 20 kopecks, equal to 3s. 9d., for 20 miles. This is not dear. We found the expenses, as far as Tumen, very light; after that they increased considerably. We left again at 9.30 A.M., and proceeded through some very pretty scenery, to Pororodni, which place we reached at 1 P.M., with four horses, the distance being twenty-five versts from our last station. Here we lunched.

At first starting we felt rather nervous at going downhill, as the drag we used was about the most clumsy piece of iron we had ever seen, and did not give us much comfort as to its restraining powers, we fully expecting it to go to bits at every hill.

The yemschik, or coachman, took us at a tremendous pace downhill, and so gave an impetus to the vehicle which nearly took it up to the top of the next one. To hear our old wheels going, every particle of the trap in a quiver, certainly required a little nerve at first to make us quite enjoy it. When firmly wedged in we always found ourselves with our heads lower than our heels. Our legs, which were encased in all manner of coverings, were so bulky and useless that we used to get them helplessly jammed in the boot of the trap, and always had difficulty to extricate them when we arrived at the post station.

One thing which soon gave us confidence was that the little spirited horses never fail; they put down their heads, whisk their tails, and bound away with a wild scamper as if they fully enjoyed the fun. I am sure the driver, who had no power over them, trusted entirely to Providence to escape any accident.

246   A LAND JOURNEY FROM

CHAPTER VIII.

We arrive at the River Selinga and cross it by the Ferry Boat—The town of Selenginsk—Disgusting Condition of the Post-house—We find a Friend—The intense Cold as we proceed to Obokunztske—The splendid State of the Snow Roads, and the Pace of our Tarantass, especially downhill—Gaps in the Road and Jumps in our Conveyance—We arrive at Sichanonar—We skirt along the Lake Baikal—Sudden Storms upon this Lake — The splendid Scenery—We pass through fine Pine Forests—Mechia—The Site of a Battle Field between the Poles and Russians—Reports of the dismal Condition of the Roads in advance—Jumping the Sledges over Chasms in the Road—Sudden Change from Calm to a terrific Storm on the Lake.

At 2.30 P.M. we proceeded on again, with four horses; the country being very hilly and heavy. The river Selinga, which we had to cross, we soon arrived at, and found that although it was partially frozen over, we could not cross it, so had to have our traps and horses placed in large boats. The operation took us twenty minutes. The boat is allowed to drift with a very swift current to the other side, the crew rowing with flat pieces of wood, and so guiding its progress. We reached the opposite bank without difficulty, and paid a rouble for the passage; and after a rapid drive over roads partially covered with snow we arrived at the small town of Selenginsk at 3.30 P.M., twenty versts from the last station.

We drove through the town, which is beautifully situated in a valley surrounded by lofty mountains, and looks clean and prosperous, and possesses the usual church, with its lofty spires and domes.

Arriving at the post station, to our chagrin we found we could not get any horses until morning. This was a foretaste of the various delays we were doomed to meet with during our journey through Siberia. It was only then 3.30 P.M.; what were we to do with ourselves? We inquired for private horses, but there were none. The post had come in before us and of course took precedence; it had taken all the horses available. It struck me, from what we saw later on, further in Siberia, that the post stations, as far as Irkoutsk, are not properly kept, as at some stations, beyond Irkoutsk, we found as many as sixty horses.

We were wondering what to do to pass the time, Mr. Walcott and myself having come to the conclusion that to remain in the post station was an impossibility, the atmosphere being simply disgusting—I should think it must have been months since a window had been opened, and already at that early hour travellers were sleeping on the ground, half undressed, and looking very dirty—when an invitation, written in very good English, came for us, from a Russian gentleman whose acquaintance we had made in Kiachta and who had heard of our arrival. At first we thought of declining, as our appearance was anything but presentable, but while we were debating our kind friend came round and took us all three with him. We had noticed a fine-looking house, on our entrance into the town, and this proved to be the residence we were invited to.

We were introduced to the lady of the house and found a small and friendly company, which in Russia is most sociable and enjoyable. No absurd restraints, everybody knows everybody, and music, singing, dancing—in fact anything is indulged in calculated to keep up a constant flow of innocent amusement.

We soon recognised several faces we had seen in Kiachta, and were most warmly greeted by some young Russian artillery officers whose acquaintance we had made; and very well informed gentlemen they were. The usual amount of eating and drinking followed, and we performed our share heartily.

Some very quaint national songs were sung with great effect, and our host, who played the piano very well, discussed a sonata, accompanied by a Russian officer on the violin.

Before bidding a final adieu to all these kind friends, we visited the quarters of the Russian artillery officers, and were presented with photographs, and, what was very valuable to us, some capital tobacco. At last we made our farewells, and strolled away to the station; and awfully cold it was.

My friend had determined to sleep in the tarantass, preferring to run the risk of being frozen, to breathing the foul atmosphere in the post station; but I was rather afraid of doing so; I soon found however that I could not stand it; a quantity of new arrivals were strewed about on the ground, and the stench was intolerable, so I also slept in the tarantass, taking the precaution to wrap myself well up; and we were only awoke in the morning by the horses being harnessed in. We found every breath had frozen and formed a coating of ice upon the wrappers we had covered over our faces; whiskers, beard, and moustaches frozen hard, and forming spikes as sharp as a pin. It was very cold as we faced the wind at 4 A.M.

A rapid drive brought us at eight o'clock to the small station of Arbotscke—distance 25 versts; fare (4 horses), 1 rouble 62 kopecks. Changing horses here, and drinking lots of hot tea, which we always found preferable to spirits—in fact spirits are too potent for the clear ozone one inhales, as the least thing in the shape of strong drink mounts to the head—we bowled away along a capital road, passing through a beautiful and hilly country to Obokunztske, where we dined at twelve o'clock, making a capital meal out of our joint stock of provisions. We had a sort of soup, called *pillmania*, composed of small balls of suet filled with meat, but it used to produce such violent indigestion that we gave it up. The sun had come out, the wind had fallen, and the temperature became quite pleasant. We fully enjoyed the scenery, and the novelty of the life we were passing. Such a splendid atmosphere; the sky looked the purest blue I have ever seen, the frost hanging on the trees, gently falling like spangles to the ground, glittering in the sun as the breeze passed through the branches. The snow, which was becoming thicker as we advanced, promised well for sledging. Every hill was clearly marked in the horizon and sharply defined. How could we help feeling happy, and enjoying thoroughly all we saw and did? How different from the old hackneyed tourist routes, crowded with travellers, all bent on seeing the same old sights again—nothing of adventure, nothing new! With us everything was bright, we were learning at every turn something fresh.

We found at Obokünztske that the postmaster and family were about to dine, so as we had not with us too large a stock of provisions we requested to be allowed to share their dinner, and a capital one it was, to us. Soup, called *Tzchee*, composed of vegetables, a little milk (*moloko*), and a huge lump of meat, formed a meal of itself; the cutlets which followed, doubtless, in a country where plenty is always found would be considered rather queer food, as they were of an immense size (which we rather appreciated), and uncommonly greasy—I have no doubt but that, were they offered us now, we should refuse to face them; a peculiar sort of cabbage, soaked in a very inferior kind of lamp-oil, followed, but, although we had long ago got over all daintiness, we could not manage to swallow any of it. This sumptuous repast cost the three of us, and also the dinner for Colonel B.'s two servants, three roubles, or 9*s.*; not dear, considering the country we were in.

Much comforted, we jumped, or rather rolled, into our tarantass again; it was no easy matter, cumbered as we were with furs, to climb into our ancient vehicle. I used generally to take a header in, and when nearly suffocated get tolerably fixed.

We enjoyed very much the rapid drive to Botkara, twenty-five versts, which we accomplished in two hours and a half. We proceeded onwards, with as little delay as possible, and travelled over a great deal of snow, which we hailed with much pleasure, looking forward to soon being able to sledge. Just as we started from Botkara our horses bolted, and took us straight up against a house—fortunately with but little damage, which was soon repaired with rope. We crossed the Selinga again, this time on the ice, and drove into Nijni Oudinsk at 8.30 A.M., down a hill, at a pace which took away our breath. Colonel B—— took us to a house belonging to a servant of his, as he had business here, and we were to wait for him; this we found a pleasant rest after the shaking we had endured. Every bone in my body felt sore, and I was altogether very much fatigued. The only drawback was that the rooms, as usual, were intolerably hot.

We had been passing through a most beautiful country before arriving at Nijni Oudinsk, with everywhere increasing signs of cultivation and prosperity. The scenery in the neighbourhood of the river Selinga is very fine indeed; the banks are lined with lofty hills, covered with pine forests. As we crossed over the ice, the sun, which had become obscured by passing clouds, gave a gloomy grandeur to the scene which was highly impressive. All the villages we had seen were clean, and composed of strong log-houses, something like Swiss chalets, the better ones having beautifully carved fronts. The peasantry seemed rich and prosperous, and being so few in number—some 300,000 in all Siberia—have plenty of room to get on, without interfering with each other.

We found nearly all the post stations as far as Nijni Oudinsk very tidy and pleasant, but intolerably close and stuffy. The postmasters, without exception, were most obliging. We had heard so much to the contrary that we were agreeably surprised to find ourselves so well treated; but some who travel make a point of seeing everything in the worst light, never being contented, and making themselves as obnoxious as they can. In an account of a similar journey to this through Siberia, written by an English traveller, we found various lamentations as to the miseries endured, and various delays on the route. That journey was undertaken at about the worst time in the year, in the autumn, when the rivers are only commencing to freeze, but sometimes enough to make ferry communication difficult; the roads are at that time in a dreadful condition, as they are left to themselves some time before the snow forms. Any traveller who would make this route must make up his mind to take things as they come, and not groan and grumble at everything. It must also be remembered that Siberia, until very lately, was nearly unknown to Europeans and that even now very small portions have been explored. Another thing I read in the account referred to was, that the writer, at one of the post stations, found a Polish postmaster who was delighted to see an Englishman, and—no doubt, poor fellow, never imagining his conversation would appear in print—entered into a political discussion. As the book was translated into Russian I fear the unfortunate postmaster is now expiating his rashness, in misplacing confidence in a stranger, in one of the mines. I heard a good deal and I saw a great deal on my way through Siberia, but I do not think I have any right either to introduce conversations entered into in confidence or to criticise the people I sojourned with, sneer at their manners, or return ingratitude for all the kindness we received wherever we went. When I commenced my homeward route I made up my mind to find travelling very difficult, so do not feel at all justified at indulging in retrospective grumblings. I perfectly confess that the method of getting over the ground, especially in the tarantass, was anything but agreeable, and I felt it enough to make me sometimes very miserable; but for all that, I do not see why I should enter into violent diatribes against everybody and every thing in the country.

As far as we had gone we found no difficulty in getting horses—of course this was all due to our being in company with Colonel B——; and travelling was very cheap.

We always found on showing our *podorojna*—or postal blank—that we were at once provided with horses. Our pass only stipulated that we were to have three horses, as the government regulations are particular as to keeping horses always ready for post communication and carriers, but we were nearly always able to obtain four or five as required, paying only for three or four, never for more.

Having servants with us, they generally started

before we did, and so, reaching the next station sooner, we found horses waiting for us and the samovar boiling, tea already made, and thus were saved much time.

Happily all our luggage consisted of flat leathern bags, and so, with a thin mattress over them, and being well wrapped up, we were, I am sure, more comfortable than the Colonel, who however did not seem to care much, probably being accustomed to it.

It is impossible to place any luggage at the back of the vehicle, as, although there is generally a place for it, even if tied on with the strongest cord it would soon be cut off and stolen. The sun only rose about 9°, so we had not much daylight; it set at 3.30 P.M. The horses we used were small but very strong, and trot along at any pace.

We had only time to change our clothes and get a limited wash—our supply of water being confined to a tea-kettle, which shed a few drops into the palms of the hands and is thence transferred to the face. The Colonel, who in travelling costume hardly did justice to his appearance, came out an unlimited swell, in evening coat, &c., with plenty of decorations, when lots of friends who had heard of his arrival came to pay their respects, &c., and of course then commenced the usual amount of eating, drinking, and smoking, until our rooms, which we were to sleep in, became unbearable. Finding we could not get any ventilation by means of windows, we resorted to an artifice; we took it in turns, when nobody was paying attention, to open the outer door, and although of course it was soon discovered and shut, still it gave a breath of air; but the owner of the house, who ought to have been a stoker, supplied the huge stove from time to time with armfuls of huge logs of wood, so that when our various friends departed our apartments were like a Turkish bath, and full of tobacco smoke. But after travelling in the tarantass, although we had no beds, but only the floor to lie down upon, we soon managed to get to sleep; and when we woke up in the morning, the fire having gone out in the stove, we found everything hard frozen and bitterly cold.

There is not much to see at Nijni Oudinsk. It is a small clean-looking town, containing about 4000 inhabitants; the houses are well built, mostly of wood. It has a good market-place, and four churches of some architectural pretensions. A few troops were quartered there. It was too cold to walk about, but it certainly would not take one hour to see the whole place.

S

Colonel B—— having finished all he had to do we started again at 3 P.M. of the 25th in sledges, as there had been a good fall of snow, quite sufficient to form a good road. Another officer in a Cossack regiment joined us here, so we had three vehicles, and most primitive ones they were; they seemed, with the exception of the wooden runners, to be composed of small sticks, matting, and ropes, and it was a wonder they held together at all.

Mr. Walcott and myself travelled in one sledge, the Colonel and Cossack officer in another, and the two servants in the third. We had to arrange our baggage again as well as we could. Our sledge was quite open. The motion of the sledge, after the tarantass, was delightful as we glided along over a smooth hard road at a rapid but hardly perceptible pace.

We proceeded for some distance on the River Selenga, and then, crossing over to the left bank, we struck inland away from it. We were in the act of becoming most enthusiastic about sledging as compared with other modes of travelling, and stating that it would be a long time ere we became tired of it, when our faith was roughly shaken, for all of a sudden, without the slightest notice, over we went. Luckily, we were going rather slowly, and so we managed to stick in the sledge by holding on hard to the sides and to each other until the horses were pulled in. We however began to think that if this were to be part of the fun it would become a rather seriously unpleasant state of affairs before reaching Nijni Novgorod. Of course we were now kept on the alert, and it was well we were, as we had not gone far when over we tipped again, and this time we were going at a good pace. The yemschik was thrown, but somehow or other we managed to grasp the reins, and after going some distance to stop the horses.

We really began to feel somewhat alarmed now, and we debated what we should do, but as we had only gone half-way to the next station, and the other two sledges were far ahead, and we could not make the drivers understand a word we said, we had to submit to being righted again, and proceeded onwards, feeling very uncomfortable.

A little way on we came to the top of a very steep hill. Nothing will stop a sledge once launched at a good pace downhill, so away we went at a tremendous pace, but not far before over we went a third time, and were on this occasion shot out against a bank. Being wrapped up in so many coverings saved us from being much hurt, but we were much shaken. The coachman was thrown, and we could see the sledge on one side bowling away downhill at an awful pace, and it was only stopped by running into a cart at the bottom. We were neither of us generally given to feeling nervous, but we certainly did not care about entering the sledge again, which, however, as we were near the next station, we did, and proceeded slowly there. Of course all our delightful anticipations of the comfort of sledging had vanished. On arriving at Polowinger—thirty versts, at six o'clock, fare 1 rouble 50 kopecks—we immediately informed the Colonel, who, however, did not seem to think much of it. We examined our sledge and found that one of the long fenders, which project from the side and alone kept the vehicle from overturning, was broken; this immediately accounted for our mishaps, so procuring some good strong rope we had it well repaired, and somewhat doubtingly got in again, and reached without accident Elinga—twenty-three versts, fare 1 rouble—at 9 P.M. ; but on our way to Tarakanopsky, where we arrived at 10.30 P.M., we again turned over. So we now made up our minds that unless something was done we would wait for another sledge, and not risk our necks any longer. Finding we could not get any new fenders there, we arranged to post as the servants had done, handing them our sledge. It entailed our taking a fresh one every station, but as we kept our baggage in the old sledge we found it not at all disagreeable, as all our wraps were always arranged for us. But the sledges were very small and did not give much room for the legs. So we arrived at Kábanst at 2.30 A.M., without further mishap, on the 26th of November. Here we changed our sledge and began to experience the pleasure of gliding along at from ten to fifteen miles per hour, especially as we felt quite safe. Taking a short cut, avoiding a station, thereby saving fifteen versts, we reached Posolskoi, at 8.30 A.M.

This station is situated on the Lake Baikal, or, as it is more commonly called by the peasantry, la mer Sainte. The Mongols call it Bai hol, meaning lake of fire. It is supposed to have been formed by an extinct volcano. It is in its narrowest place 30 miles across and about 400 miles long. It is said that soundings in the centre have never yet been obtained. Surrounded by lofty hills and mountains on all sides, and narrowing and widening at various intervals, it is liable to fearful storms, which come on very suddenly, especially towards winter, and the navigation is considered very dangerous and difficult. Large waves roll in like those at sea, on to the shore.

Before arriving at the station we were undecided whether to cross by the steamer or by the new road round the lake, which had, however, been mostly destroyed by the great inundations in the autumn, and was not considered safe; but on getting there—and bitterly cold it was, 20° or more below zero; I thought I had lost my nose and ears, as they were quite dead; a little longer, I am sure they would have been frozen—we were informed that we could not go round the lake, but must wait for the steamer, whose movements were most uncertain. One of the steamers had been recently burnt, so there was only one now—and such a craft!—an old crazy barge, of a design certainly before Noah's time! Her last trip, seventy-two miles, she did in five days! Once she had taken thirteen, as when it blows off the shore she can neither approach nor land her passengers. Her rate of speed, with an enormous consumption of wood, was, I believe, at most, two knots per hour; and her snorting could be heard miles away; and more dirty or wretched accommodation it would be difficult to conceive.

It is curious that with the direct traffic from China to Russia passing this route there never should have been good steamers. They would have paid well. Of course, now that the Suez Canal is open, most of the tea will take that route to Russia, and divert much of the traffic. But such an odd-looking craft as the *General* something was (I forget the name now) I shall never forget. The station was full of people, and it was some time before we could get the samovar. The heat was rather welcome this time, as I was most miserably frozen. My fingers and toes were in fearful pain. Walcott's nose was slightly frost-bitten and he suffered much from it afterwards.

Whilst we were debating as to what we were to do and wondering how we could pass the time and how we could exist in the dirty station of Posolskoi, waiting, perhaps for days, until the steamer left, some new arrivals put us at our ease, they just having come by the new route round the lake. They, however, gave us a dismal account of the state of the roads, telling us to prepare to encounter some really dangerous incidents, which were not at all exaggerated, as we found out afterwards.

But anything was preferable to remaining where we then were; so after a very short debate, in which we all agreed without discussion, we decided to depart at once and try our luck. We were very glad to go this way, as the route is little known and it was something new.

Having made up our minds to start by this route we at once ordered horses, which after a short delay we obtained, three for each sledge. I do not think I shall ever forget the cold. A strong north-east wind was blowing right in our teeth, which, although we were well wrapped up and faces covered, it was impossible to keep out. We proceeded for about an hour on the borders of the lake. It was hard frozen, and I think at the rate we went we must have done fully thirteen miles in the hour, as we reached Goltomensky at ten o'clock, after a drive of an hour and fifteen minutes, the distance being twenty-five versts. On arriving at the station, quickly changing horses, we proceeded over a capital road at splendid speed. The snow on the road being as smooth as a billiard board, the sledge once launched downhill nothing will stop its progress; so on arriving at the summit of one of the many undulations in the road, the driver giving a whoop, away go the horses, full of excitement, downhill, and with impetus enough to reach the top of the opposite one. I must confess my first feeling was a rather nervous one, and I experienced a very curious sensation, at dipping down nearly perpendicularly one moment, which made it difficult for us to avoid being pitched out of the sledge, and then rattling away as hard as we could go up the opposite hill, looking straight up to the skies, which nearly sent us out of the back, the speed taking away our breath. It took us several of these dips, which occurred very often during our journey round the Lake Baikal, before we became accustomed to the motion. However, after having shot a few of these extraordinary gaps in the road, we gained confidence, and fully entered into the excitement of the speed we were travelling at as the sense of danger disappeared.

We arrived at Sichanonar at twelve o'clock; distant fifteen versts, fare 1 rouble 20 kopeks for four horses. Here we dined, and enjoyed it very much. Nothing like this sort of travelling for good and healthy appetites! After leaving this station, we skirted along the Lake Baikal, and we could well imagine that fearful storms come upon it suddenly. The waves, like those breaking in from the ocean, were rolling in with sullen roar upon the beach, and dark heavy clouds were hanging over the mountain tops; the whole forming from the height a grand and imposing appearance. The woods and mountains which we were passing through were covered with snow, and the branches of the trees were bent to the ground with the weight of frozen snow which clung to them. Large blocks of ice, confusedly tossed on the waves of the lake, washed towards the shore, and became frozen in masses and formed miniature icebergs—a sublime and picturesque scene such as we never before or since have looked upon.

As we proceeded the scenery continued fine, and the roads being good we began to scout the idea of the difficulties we had heard so much about, and we gave ourselves up to the comfort of the sledge and the exhilarating excitement of the speed with which we were driving through the fresh and bracing air.

The pace at times was truly tremendous, but we now felt no alarm as to the capabilities of the sledge, as we were provided at each station with a good one. The road, which at this part of the lake is carried along the edge of a precipice, is only wide enough at places for a single sledge.

It becomes at various intervals very bad, full of holes, and as there were no fences on the side, a false step would soon have hurled us over the mountain.

Passing through some magnificent pine forests we arrived at a small station, the name of which I forget, at three o'clock, and after changing horses proceeded onwards. The road we had to pass over was very deep with fresh-fallen snow, and at times our sledge, although drawn by five horses, was with difficulty pulled through the heavy drifts, which were nearly two feet deep. This very much retarded our progress, so that we did not arrive at Mechia, twenty-five versts, before six o'clock. This station is famous for a great battle which was fought on the spot some years ago, between the Poles and Russians, resulting in a victory for the latter.

Here, as usual, we refreshed and warmed the inner man with the usual quantity of tea and cigarettes, and here we were entertained with dismal reports as to the condition of the road before us. The difficulties which we found were not at all exaggerated; for after leaving Mechia, we made a steep descent on to the lake, and we had then to skirt along its borders, over some very awkward bits, the roads having here been in places entirely destroyed; and it was only by jumping the horses, sledge and all, at full speed over the various chasms on the road, that we managed to surmount what seemed to us, as we approached them, insurmountable obstacles.

At last the road became so bad and dangerous that although it was freezing to any extent, and we had to divest ourselves of some of our wraps, we got out of our sledges and walked a bit. The wind, the enemy we most feared, had died away; and now, as we walked along close to the lake, it appeared as calm as glass; overhead, a clear cloudless sky, with hundreds of bright stars, shining each with its own distinct refulgency; not a sound beyond the whoop of our driver was heard to disturb the silence, nor a living being beyond ourselves in sight. Lofty mountains, with their pine-clad crests towering to the heavens confusedly in gigantic forms, proudly defiant with their snowy breasts, as if conscious of their own magnificence and strength, surrounded us on all sides.

I must confess that notwithstanding the cold, and although weary with trudging through the deep snow, covered with furs, &c., I could not resist the feeling of intense awe and wonder which came over me as the scene gradually grew into my senses. Although it was night, still the air was clear and bright, and every star gave a reflection of its own, which made everything as visible as if it were day. But to prove how quick changes occur in this lake, even while I was dreaming and wondering whether heaven could be like the scene before us, where no storms arise and calms abide for ever—black clouds, as if by magic, stole over and obscured the scene ; the wind began to move the branches of the trees, and cause heavy balls of snow to fall about us, and the lake, which just before was so tranquil,

> Bore wave on wave, lashed forward by the breeze.

In a moment the tops of the mountains disappeared, enveloped in deepest gloom, and all we could hear was the groaning of the forest trees as they swayed about, shaken by the mighty wind, and the sullen boom of the waters thrown upon the stony beach. Of course this necessitated a halt, as it was too dark to venture along the road, as it would have been only too easy to drive into the lake, and its depth is too well known to have made it anything but an agreeable prospect. But very soon the stars shone forth again, the clouds rolled heavily away, and beyond a small addition to our incumbrances, in the shape of a coating of fresh-fallen snow, and the agitation of the lake, which had not yet subsided, we should hardly have been able to imagine that a storm had come and gone with such marvellous rapidity. But all this time we were becoming congealed, and sentimentality, although very refreshing in a genial climate, unfortunately did not prevent us from returning again to the reality of our existence, and lamenting the absence of all sense of feeling in our feet, and giving way to the doleful feeling that our toes were frozen and would probably remain in our boots when we took them off; and for days afterwards we suffered from the freezing we got that night. We proceeded over a rather better bit of road and reached the next station at twelve o'clock. It was a nice new and clean building, as indeed, are all the post stations on the Baikal. The road ahead being very bad, and the cold intense, it was deemed advisable to wait here a few hours for the moon, and we were not at all sorry to wrap ourselves up in our cloaks and lie down upon the floor before the stove, as we had not been able to indulge in much sleep lately, it not being easy to do so in a sledge or in the intense cold. We here learnt that we were the first who had passed over this route, towards Irkoutsk since the inundations, but a few had come the opposite direction.

CHAPTER IX.

Intensity of the Cold—Horrible State of the Roads, and dangerous Situation of our Sledges—We reach Murmske—The Beauty of the Scenery at this part of the Lake Baikal—We arrive at Mouradeofsky, and strike inland—We cross a Branch of the River Angara, the last River to freeze in Siberia—Irkoutsk, the capital Town of Eastern Siberia—We replenish our Clothing and Stores—The Landlord of our Hotel attempts to delay us—Drunkards sentenced to keep the snow Roads in order—We make the Acquaintance of a Russian Officer, who agrees to travel with us to St. Petersburg—Russian Fashions with respect to Dress—Polish Exiles at Irkoutsk—The Gold and Silver Mines of Siberia—Terrible Nature of the Convict Labour, chiefly for political Offences—Enormous Riches of Owners of these Mines—The Government Mines furnish the Emperor's Income—The various Tribes in the Neighbourhood of Lake Baikal—Different Methods of Salutation observed during our Route—A first-rate Restaurant—Dilatory Nature of the Town People.

At 3 A.M. of the 27th of November, very loth indeed to move, we made a start again. I had been dreaming all manner of pleasant things, and it did seem hard to turn out again into the bitter cold and only half awake. However, we managed to doze at intervals through a very heavy snowstorm, which covered us in our open sledge about four inches and was most disagreeable. We made the best of it, although we felt intensely aggrieved. Fancy the snow pelting against one's face, melting by our breath and then freezing again; it certainly was not pleasant. The horses were all covered with icicles and looked like magnified hedgehogs. Our whiskers and moustaches became bristles, and would have cut any one who should have chanced to run against us. We arrived at a small station at 5 A.M., and a general rush was made by the contents of our two sledges to secure the best place near the stove, and there a general thaw commenced, and various groans as to the inclemency of the weather and the roads before us.

Warmed again by the beverage of the teetotaler, we started once more. We really did feel grateful that the snow had ceased to fall, but it had made the road very heavy. We passed over some awful places on the road and were obliged to walk a good deal, which half froze us, having twice to turn out of our warm wraps; but how the sledge managed to go over huge rocks, large gaps in the road, and blocks of timber, trees, &c., and not get capsized into the lake was a wonder, but doubtless very much due to the skill and judgment of our driver. The road at this portion of the lake had been entirely destroyed. The telegraph posts

T

had been also swept away but had been renewed again.

Arriving at Snier Ziga, or "station of snow," eighteen versts from the last station, we made our lunch, and it was a necessity for all of us, as we were feeling quite done up. I never felt much the desire for strong drink, as I have before stated, the atmosphere supplies its want; but I must say just then I would have given much for a small glass of brandy. But then we had none, and at that time I had not accustomed myself to swallow the strong Russian spirit. The first time I took a glass it entirely took away my breath and rendered me speechless for some time.

Leaving again, we continued for some distance to skirt along the sides of the lake, the road for a short way being rather better; but it soon disappeared and we had to take the old road, which certainly, if not dangerous, looked so. We had some tremendous ascents and descents to make without any railings at the side of the road, which was only wide enough for one sledge, and was not made more convenient by the telegraph posts being placed in the centre, so that we had always, in order to pass them, to send one side of the sledge up on the bank. I really did begin to think that if this sort of road was to go on much longer we might consider ourselves very lucky to accomplish our journey safely, as I am convinced we indulged in a succession of the narrowest shaves; and although the old maxim, that a miss is as good as a mile, is quite true, it did not make us feel quite happy. It is a great strain on the nerves to be constantly going through these perils, one of which per diem would be quite enough for the ordinary traveller. What I used always to dread was coming suddenly to the top of a hill. We, being in the foremost sledge, on looking down could see the narrow road turning sharp corners, with no manner of railing to keep us from going over the precipice. We had to go full speed in order to avoid being run over by the two sledges which came rattling down hard behind us. Had one of the horses fallen it certainly would have been all up with us in a very brief space of time.

It came on to snow heavily again, and we were nearly smothered, but luckily this time it was freezing so hard that it did not melt, and we did not get as before a regular mask of ice; but it was most trying.

The scenery all along from the last station was

magnificent; splendid woods on each side. Now and then we would catch glimpses of the opposite bank as the clouds rolled off the lofty mountains. We reached Murmske at two o'clock and proceeded onwards without delay. The weather improved but the cold increased, our thermometer marking 62° of frost. We had to walk two miles of the way, as the road took us by the lake and was too dangerous for us to remain in our sledges. We reached the small station of Oŭ-tŭ-Leek at half-past eight and left again at nine.

We had some more disagreeable hills to pass over, the road being unpleasantly narrow. But it was a splendid night, and although there was no moon the wind had died away and the stars shone brightly. The lake was perfectly calm, the lofty pines glistened, with their branches laden with frost; the air was clear and cold, and the bells on our horses rang merrily as we rattled away—the drivers shouting and we comfortably wrapped up. It really was most enjoyable, and after all worth all the trouble we had taken to see such really charming scenery, and which I do not suppose could be found of equal and similar beauty in any other portion of the globe. What a great idea one gets through travelling over strange countries of the grandeur and magnificence of the Creator!

At 2.30 P.M. of the 28th we arrived at Mouradeofsky, called after a former governor of Siberia. After leaving this station the road became much better, and we struck inland away from the lake and followed a tolerably flat plain for about sixteen hours, when we reached another small station at 6 P.M. There we were much delayed for want of horses, so had to remain, much to our annoyance, until eight o'clock. We then proceeded to Botshiegobolsky, which we reached after a splendid drive, having passed through a large village and crossed a wide frozen river, a branch of the Angara, a little further on re-crossing it, and at 3.30 P.M. we entered the village of Vijenski.

This is a long straggling village, and has a curious wooden church with green domes. This was the last station before Irkoutsk, where we intended remaining a few days to make arrangements for continuing our journey. We were not at all sorry, as after the hardships we had gone through in consequence of the roughness of the roads, a rest was becoming absolutely necessary. Losing no time, as we were anxious to reach Irkoutsk as early as possible, we started off again—a long road as narrow as a bowling alley, over which our sledge glided at a rapid pace. Of course, when one is in a hurry even the greatest speed seems slow, and this last part of the journey did seem interminable. We were delayed some time on the banks of the Angara, which was not yet frozen over, waiting for the ferry. I believe the Angara is generally the last river to freeze in the winter in Siberia. But at last we could discern the approach of the ferry through the heavy steam which was rising from the river and clinging to us as it froze. The ferry was a sort of a large floating bridge, worked by ropes from the other side. Five sledges, horses, men and all, crossed on it, and it was large enough for more. At last we reached Irkoutsk, and drove up to the *Hôtel Amour* at 7.30 P.M.

Although to the European traveller this barrack of a building, magnificently called an hotel, would probably appear miserable and dirty, to us it was a splendid affair. We found sofas—beds are unknown —and also are washing apparatus in the rooms. We got a good dinner, consisting of magnificent large sized cutlets and a decoction called Madeira, which however we very much enjoyed; and after having had a Russian bath we retired to our sofas, which were the only approach to a bed that we had seen since leaving Pekin, and slept until late next morning.

On the 29th, when we rose from a refreshing slumber, which had entirely done away with the fatigue of our journey, the thermometer stood at 40° below zero, or 72° of frost; so it may be imagined how awfully cold it was. Our first care was to purchase each a good long pelisse lined with fur (called *schubes* by the Russians), some very thick gloves lined with skin like mittens, and a cap something like a grenadier's, made of Astracan, which I could pull right over my face.

We also ordered some socks made of goat skin and some high felt boots. The cold there was so intense that it seizes hold of one's nose, ears, fingers, &c., in a second, and frost-bites frequently occur.

We made the acquaintance of several Russian officers, who kindly showed us about and told us what to do, &c. But we did not see much of the town at one time, as it was too cold to drive about much.

We at once began to look for a suitable sledge, but without success. We afterwards found out that there were plenty, but our landlord was not anxious to part with us so soon, so kept that fact from us.

We also inquired if any Russian officers, who at that time of the year go a great deal to St. Petersburg, were likely to be found, but without success.

I advise any one strongly who may travel through Siberia to make up his mind to take things easy. It is no use being in a hurry, as that aspect of affairs is utterly unknown in Siberia. I never saw such people for procrastination. Do to-morrow what you can do to-day, should be their motto. However, as we did not expect to do much in one day we were not disappointed.

When we rose on the morning of the 30th, notwithstanding the presence of a huge stove in our rooms, everything was hard frozen and the cold was most disagreeable; we only ventured out for a short distance, and were glad to return and place ourselves as near the stove as possible. But I must say that Irkoutsk is not an interesting place, and one drive through it is quite sufficient. The streets are wide and clean, and the houses, built of wood, and a few stone ones, are good; but there are no public buildings worth seeing. While we were there an exhibition of machinery, produce, &c., was being held by the inhabitants. This exhibition was considered very good. I must say it reminded me very much of a show in a country fair.

They have a capital way of keeping the roads in order there. Any one found drunk in the streets by way of punishment has to work on them the whole of the next day; and by what I saw there must be a good many drunkards in Irkoutsk. The snow roads are kept even by cartfuls being brought in from the country and poured out on the roads, the drunken amateurs having to spread it smoothly over.

We fortunately made the acquaintance of a captain in the Russian artillery, who seemed a very nice gentlemanly man, and he agreed to go with us to St. Petersburg, thereby taking all anxiety away as to our future travelling. He was armed with a courier's pass, so that would insure speed at least. We only required a good sledge, and commenced at once active inquiries.

Irkoutsk being the capital town of Eastern Siberia the governor resides there and holds his court. Receptions take place Thursdays and Mondays, and are attended by the officers of the garrison, who must be very numerous, as we hardly saw any one else. The garrison consists of some two thousand men. Russian officers do not like being stationed in Siberia, and look upon it as a sort of exile, to be endured with as much patience as possible.

Society at Irkoutsk is very exclusive, and holds very much to itself, as is generally the case where it is limited. We were fairly astonished at the number of generals and colonels we came across, like blackberries in a hedge. A most extraordinary custom, at least so it seemed to our Anglo-Saxon ideas, was that when paying a morning visit men wore evening dress, and those who had decorations wore them also; whereas in the evening, at a ball, they wore morning dress—exactly reversing our ideas. We were proceeding to pay our respects to a certain general when a friend met us and asked to see how we were dressed. It was rather insulting to be told (because we had taken some trouble in our attire) that we could not pay the intended visit in morning dress; so we had to return and put on evening costume. This prevented us making the acquaintances we otherwise should have done, as we had no inclination to drive about in dress clothes all day.

A great number of Poles reside in Irkoutsk, who have been exiled from their own fair land. They only manage to exist by following trades or some menial occupations. They are mostly men of education and family, and many of them were formerly rich, but when they are exiled they lose all rank and social standing. They have no names, and all their property becomes confiscated to the crown. They cannot bear witness in court, in fact socially they cease to exist; and a fine race of men they are as a rule.

Austria has given her Polish subjects entire freedom, whilst Russia holds hers still degraded and enslaved. Russian Poland includes 18,000,000 inhabitants. There is no doubt but that the sufferings of the Poles may be attributed very much to the continual plots and disturbances against the Russian government. With the greatest sympathy for the Poles, I cannot help feeling that it would be wiser and happier for them to acquiesce, however hard and degrading it may be, in what must ever be their existence. Russia intends to keep Poland and gradually Russianise it.

There are also a great many Russian exiles at Irkoutsk undergoing banishment for various political offences. A perfect system of espionage is kept up, so that it would be impossible for one of these unfortunate people to quit the town or do anything without its being known. Irkoutsk contains in all a population of 30,000.

It is calculated that in Eastern Siberia alone there are at least thirty to forty thousand Polish political exiles; but they are kept in different portions for fear of disturbances, a great many having to work in the mines—a species of forced labour especially dreaded. Many a Pole of gentlemanly education and good family has been condemned to this dreadful labour; and no wonder that, to deaden their senses and forget their existence, they take to drinking the horrible spirits made in the country, and die drunkards.

There is as little to see in the neighbourhood of Irkoutsk as there is in it. About forty versts away there is a large manufactory of crockery, glass, and all kinds of knicknacks, called *tietsienske*. This is a curiosity for Siberians, but hardly for European travellers.

I do not think it would be out of place at this portion of my book to give a slight description of the mines in Siberia and the different races of people. I have compiled a small map which shows the situation of the gold and silver mines. It was a subject I studied carefully and I think the information, &c., I received were correct. All the gold mines in Altai, about one hundred in all, with the exception of twenty-seven, belong to and are worked by the Russian government. The twenty-seven were given to great functionaries, and they let them out again to merchants. For example, at the mines of Sierra, Marientzky, a merchant of Yenesech, pays yearly to the Duke of —— 3000 roubles for each 40 lbs. weight. In this mine it is calculated at least 1440 lbs. of gold remains. The merchant has to give all his gold to government, which in return gives him bills payable at different dates at the treasury, less the crown tax, which I believe is 25 per cent.

As a rule, the crown mines are not so good or productive as the private ones, attributable, most likely, to the jobbery which exists in them. The mines of Viechem and Olexina were formerly governmental, but so badly managed as to yield no profit. No sooner however did they pass into private hands than they yielded immense fortunes. The mines of Enissigk Taygar have yielded already 6000 pouds (a poud is 40 lbs.) and are not yet exhausted; and the rivers Sereghkind, Chorma, and Ognya have also up to the present yielded 2000 and 3000 pouds each.

The proprietors of the gold mines, accustomed to enormous fortunes, spend their money with a prodigality hardly to be conceived. They do not deny themselves anything they fancy, let the expense be ever so fabulous. A merchant, well known in Siberia, made out of his mines in a short period 40,000,000 roubles, equal to nearly £7,000,000 sterling. This he soon spent, and became bankrupt for over £1,000,000.

The silver mines are mostly governmental; a few belong to merchants. Situated in Buchlarnartal and in Nertschinsk, they are all very abundant in supply. It is stated that the officials who superintend the working of the silver mines make large sums of money; they are under no control, and so can easily exaggerate the working expenses. Thus the yield to the government, instead of being 25 per cent., is seldom over 5 per cent. These mines form part of the emperor's income. The head superintendence is generally given by the emperor to some relative, who contrives to make a good thing out of it.

The mines of Zizyamoosk were once the scene of a quarrel. It being reported that the superintendent had understated the yield, he, in revenge, inundated it, so that all the mining was stopped.

There are splendid copper and iron mines in Eastern Siberia, but little worked, as it is more expensive to convey the metals to towns where they could be smelted, &c., than to get manufactures direct from England. There is a mountain fifteen miles from Yenesech which, out of 40 lbs. excavated, gives 24 lbs. of iron and 4 lbs. of steel of first-rate quality.

On the River Abakan gold mines producing the best metal are being found, but not many yet, although there is evidence of abundance in the neighbourhood.

In the whole of Siberia there are only 4,000,000 inhabitants, or two men to a square mile. The extent of country is 300,000 geographical square miles. Savages still exist in Siberia. The Ostyak tribes are in the west; by the River Yenisee, the Toongose, who are quite savage; and in the north of the Yennesechs, also in Altai, the Teleotan, Syyotan, and Tartars live. These tribes live by fishing and hunting, and are innocent, harmless people. Near Irkoutsk, about the Baikal Lake, live the Bouriats, and farther east the Yackoutans; still further east the Kawoshshie, Choukchies, and quite east the Kamchadal.

The southern Siberian tribes are agriculturists; the northern, hunters. There are three iron factories in Siberia; one near the Baikal, the second by the Abakan, and the largest in Tumen. There were formerly some governmental factories in Altai, but they did not succeed. The principal agricultural produce of Siberia is flax.

One word more on the gold mines before closing this subject, which I fear has not been very interesting. The mines are badly worked and superintended. It is difficult to get the labourers, who are chiefly convicts and political exiles, to work, as they drink hard to drown dull care, and spend in winter all they earn in summer. Many of the owners are, or have been, bankrupt through their reckless extravagance and gambling. They do not like an intelligent man, as he knows too much; they prefer a drunkard. They only look to the day and let to-morrow take care of itself.

On Sunday, December the 5th, we were still at Irkoutsk, as although we had picked up a sledge as big as an omnibus, which could have been repaired in a few hours, it was not yet ready for us. We did feel heartily sick of remaining so long inactive, and the completion of our journey seemed as far off as ever.

The thermometer stood at 50° below zero. In January it goes as low as 70°. I invested in a small covering for my nose, as I had several escapes of losing it from frost-bite.

It was curious to note the habits and customs of the countries we passed through. The Chinese salutation is folding the hands together and raising them up and down several times. The Mongols hold up their thumb to salute, and to clench a bargain place their hand on the sleeve of the party they have made the bargain with. The Bouriats do much the same as the Mongols, but clench their bargains with a drink of schnapps. The Russians shake hands for everything; if friends, they kiss one another on the lips, but if only acquaintances they shake hands.

At Irkoutsk the *Amour* hotel is the best; there is another one, I believe, but from all accounts it is exceedingly bad. When saying the best, I mean the best of the bad; but after a journey like we had taken it was very comfortable. Cleanliness is unknown. There are no washhand-basins in the rooms, but once in the morning an overworked waiter, who, as far as I know, never seemed to go to bed, being the only waiter in the hotel, came round with a metal jug and basin. A few drops from the former he lets trickle on the hands, which are transferred to the face. This is all the visitor gets in the way of washing, and to do this once a day is considered the refinement of cleanliness. There are capital vapour-baths to be had in the town, but we found them very weakening, and they cannot be taken often. The dinners at the *Hôtel Amour* were so atrociously bad that we could not eat them, and I would recommend any one who may find himself at this dreary town to visit the *Polnische Gastaninske*, a first-rate restaurant, where we dined every day at four o'clock. All the officers seem to dine there, and play billiards all night afterwards; in fact, as I have said before, one sees nothing but officers everywhere in the town. We were fortunate enough to make the acquaintance of a fine old Polish gentleman, an exile, who spoke English perfectly, and had been in England formerly some time. He was kind enough to show us about the town, and assist us in procuring our outfit. Irkoutsk is a very dull place, and I never wish to be in it again. I cannot help recalling the fact that I was dismally disappointed with it, and our delay there was most annoying; but it is impossible, as I had before remarked, to do anything there in a hurry. The people seem there to do next to nothing, and the little they do they get through in a very undecided and slow manner. The only person whom I saw look really energetic was that unfortunate solitary waiter at the hotel, who was running about all day and nearly all night, and was constantly getting into a perplexed and confused condition. His invariable answer when called was, *Horoscho*, good, and *Sechass*, immediately, which, however, meant in an hour or two hence. How or where he slept was a mystery, but that he never took off his clothes or boots until age took them to himself, there is no doubt. That he also disdained cold water I am certain of. Before we left he had learnt our requirements and to understand the signs we made, and really attended to us very well—I am afraid much to the detriment of the other people who were staying in the hotel.

CHAPTER X.

The public Sledges at Irkoutsk—We kiss our male Friends and proceed—Our Russian military Fellow-traveller is immovably wedged with us in our Sledge—We find we have been robbed whilst at the last Hotel—We reach Bokara—The wedging Process in the Sledge gives us all Cramp—Our Sledge breaks down—We thaw our Noses—After travelling through a fine Country we arrive at Coûtoûlikskaya—Our Sledge takes to sliding sideways—A warm Day, only Thirty-two Degrees of Frost—Our Drag breaks as we are going down a precipitous Part of the Road—The Churches the only Buildings of Importance in the Towns we pass—My Leg nearly frost-bitten, on a Sack of frozen Soup—Our covered Sledge turned into a Stalactite Cave—Alzamayskaya—The Delights of Sledging—We are terribly bumped by Merchandise Sledges—Splendid Country for a Railroad—*The* Eastern Land Route — We travel on the frozen River Yenisee — The Town of Krasnoyarsk — Obliged to buy a new Sledge — We approach the Steppes of Baraba — A fearful Snow-storm — Method of indicating the proper Sledge Road—We take the wrong Route—A cut-throat Peasant Host.

THE sledges at Irkoutsk are very plentiful. They ply about the streets for hire like the cabs in London. They are very neat little arrangements and large enough for two, and have generally a sturdy little horse in them and go along at a brisk pace. The fare is thirty kopecks, equal to about tenpence per hour. The sledge roads last generally from the middle of November to the end of April. Snow has been known to fall there seven feet deep.

On the 6th of December we managed to get the sledges we had purchased ready by twelve o'clock, not however without many misgivings that we should still be delayed another day, as something was sure to turn up at the last moment. We had to kiss all our male acquaintances, which I must confess I did not care much about doing; but after all the kindness we had received we felt bound to accede to what is a sign of the most intimate friendship. We started punctually at twelve, and managed, three of us, a Captain ——, of the Russian artillery, and ourselves, to wedge into one sledge, not, however, without much puffing and blowing, as it was no easy task to manœuvre with the quantity of garments we had on.

Our sledge, which was covered over with matting, for which we paid forty roubles, equal to six pounds sterling, which certainly was cheap, looked like Noah's ark on slides.

We found our bill was very high for what the hotel had afforded us, and discovered we had each lost in some unaccountable manner 200 roubles, which, however, of course no one in the hotel knew anything about. We were somewhat consoled by our new travelling companion finding that he was also minus fifty roubles.

We crossed the River Selenga by a ferry-boat and proceeded to Bokara, which we reached at 1.30 P.M., the distance being fourteen versts. We left again immediately, and found we could always easily get horses, as our travelling companion had a government *paderoshne*. Arrived at Soŭnarskaya, twenty-two versts, at 3, and Thelminskaya at 5.30 P.M.; by that time we had somewhat shaken down. My place was in the middle, which I am inclined to think was the best, as it was warmest. I had to sit forward, which gave more room. The sledge was about six feet wide and seven long. We had become tolerably comfortable, with the exception of finding our arms and legs too much confined and being unable to move. I suffered awfully from cramp for the first few days. The great difficulty we had was to keep clear of each other's legs; as the sledge narrowed towards the end there was very little room, our legs being encased in so many pairs of boots of all kinds. I believe the only little ill-feeling ever engendered between us during the whole journey arose from the fact that we found we each had a leg too much, which interfered with our mutual comfort. One of my feet, from being wedged sideways between two boxes at the end of the sledge, got so painful towards the close of the journey that I began to fear that I should lose the use of it. But to resume, at the last-named station we found that our sledge already wanted repairing, one of the fenders being broken, the most necessary part of it, without which it is sure to capsize.

This was only the commencement of the numerous repairs our sledge required on the way. When we parted with it it was literally all cords and bits of wood. We had pushed on to pass these stations before dark, as the neighbourhood enjoys a very bad repute, convicts being there in large supply, who occasionally amuse themselves by stopping travellers and despoiling them of their goods; and although we were warned, I am sure neither of us could have got his revolver, as we were much too tightly wedged together. In fact, we did try for experiment, and found that two minutes at least were necessary to get hold of those weapons and be ready to use them. Before sleeping we rearranged our sledge; all the baggage in the bottom, hay over it, and then a mattress and pillows pushed well forward, which, after dinner, we really felt quite luxurious. So we got on better, with the exception of all suffering more or less during the night from violent cramps in our legs and arms, only one being able to move at the same time, and he only with his neighbours' consent. We took turns to blow our noses, as, if done simultaneously, we should have burst the sides of the sledge out.

The thermometer was 10° below zero, 42 of frost, which, after the much greater cold we had been enduring, was quite tolerable.

At Maltinskya we were delayed, there being no horses available, so slept there, which, as the room was heated up to about bath heat, was most uncomfortable, besides being constantly haunted by the unpleasant thought that our sledge was being looted, which made it necessary for one of us to pay it an occasional visit.

On the morning of the 7th, after having passed through a fine country, with magnificent scenery, and villages denoting every sign of wealth and prosperity, without any incident worth recording, we arrived at Coŭtoŭlikskaya, 157 versts from Irkoutsk, then on to Zalarinskaya, 30 versts further on, where we arrived at 1 P.M. Our course then took us over a very beautiful and hilly country, when our sledge began to show evident signs of being top-heavy, and of preferring, whenever we were spinning away down hill at an awful pace, to go sideways, which, besides being most uncomfortable, gave us all stiff necks, as we naturally turned our heads towards the side window, which was then in front. This propensity never left our vehicle, so after a time we became accustomed to it, as well as indifferent to its overbalancing on the fenders.

I felt quite warm during the day, there being only 32° of frost. Still proceeding through a wooded hilly country, we reached Thiretskaya at 3 P.M.—twenty-two versts in one hour and fifteen minutes; good going, but nervous work for novices in our ark.

Before coming to Ziminskaya, where we arrived at 6 P.M., we had to make a tremendous descent, which, looking down from the top, looked most alarming; especially as one side of the road was on a precipice and had no protecting railing. A drag, made of ropes, was brought into operation, and coiled round one of the slides. Not being strong of course it burst half way, and away we went quicker than any express train, our sledge bowling about in all directions. The impetus was so great that we only managed to pull up at the summit of the opposite hill.

It soon came on to snow, which made the roads very heavy, but at all events it made us rejoice that we had a covered sledge. Passing several stations during the night, we arrived at Thoŭlinskaya at eight next morning. I had managed to sleep through the night and only woke up in the morning; but having slid down to the end of the sledge I was nearly smothered and had to be hauled out. It was, however, some time before my legs, which were quite useless with cramp, gave any symptoms of coming to again.

The sun rose at 9.30 A.M., and set at 3 P.M.; but it was light about an hour before it rose, and there was a twilight of an hour and a half; and besides we had a splendid moon.

Thoŭlinskaya is a long straggling village, and has a very handsome church. All the villages we passed through in Siberia possess one or more fine churches. They are always the most noticeable buildings, and seem to be well cared for. The villagers all look healthy and strong, and the women are good-looking, with large black eyes. Beggars seem to be unknown, for I don't think we saw one until we entered Russia Proper.

The villages look clean and prosperous, and are well built; all the houses are made of wood.

Without any incident we reached Houdoyélanskaya at four o'clock, where we dined. We had with us a large sack of frozen soup, in slabs, called *tchee*, made of beef and vegetables, &c., and we always found it first-rate. We always carried this sack at the foot of the sledge. One night I could not make out how it was that, do what I would, my right leg became nearly frozen, although as well wrapped up as usual; however, the morning disclosed the reason: my leg had been reposing on this sack of frozen soup.

The greatest comfort, at all the stations, was the ever-boiling samovar, which produced, with the assistance of the tea we carried with us, the most refreshing beverage, on a journey like the one I am describing. The traveller must remember that in this portion of Siberia provisions or wine are seldom to be had; so he should always lay in a good supply at the small towns which are met at intervals. We carried some sherry and champagne with us, which, however, we had to thaw before drinking, as although we carried them in the warmest part of the sledge, they were always frozen to the very bottom. Perhaps an idea of the intensity of the cold may be given by the following incident, which happened on our journey.

We had purchased a bottle of what in those regions was called Madeira; a decoction which would be considered utterly undrinkable in England, being so full of spirit. After leaving the station, we had agreed to divide this bottle equally, no one to drink without the other's knowledge. The bottle was under my pillow. About twenty minutes afterwards, thinking my companions were asleep, I gently extricated the bottle, drew the cork, and raised it to my mouth, feeling very much in want of it. To my disappointment, it was frozen to the very bottom. Of course my friends, who were not asleep, had a good laugh at my expense. Some hard-boiled eggs we carried with us were frozen under our pillow in a few minutes as hard as stones.

We reached Kargatougskaya at seven, and Nijni Udinsk, a small town on the river Uda, at 9.30, having made $483\frac{3}{4}$ versts from Irkoutsk. The last two stations, as at Kiachta, are seldom visited by snow; and we had anticipated having to mount our sledges on carts; but, as good luck would have it, snow had fallen, so we were not delayed.

There being nothing to see, or delay the traveller, at Nijni Udinsk we proceeded onwards. At the station, however, feeling that great wish for beer or porter which is always so strong when not obtainable, we inquired of the postmaster if a bottle of the latter was to be had, and he provided us with one for the modest sum of three roubles—nine shillings. It was labelled " Barclay Percins "— evidently a fabrication, as the " Perkins" was misspelt; and of course it was undrinkable.

When we woke on the morning of the 9th and daylight appeared we found that we were all covered with frost. Our sledge looked like a cave, with large stalactites hanging from the roof. Horses and everything looked frosty and cold; so stopping at a large village named Alzamayskaya, we thawed and breakfasted. This was ninety-four versts from Nijni Udinsk.

We found from the experience we had already gained that the best method of travelling was to have the horses changed at each post station, with as small delay as possible, and to take our meals with all despatch. After a few days' travelling in a sledge in Siberia in the middle of winter a most intense longing possesses the traveller to get out of that part of the globe as fast as possible.

People who have never made such a journey, and consequently know nothing whatever about it, are accustomed to descant on the delights of sledging. They say nothing can be more delightful than gliding over a smooth even surface, so imperceptibly as hardly to know that you are moving. I can only recommend them to try it. Thirty to forty days and nights' continual travelling, fingers and toes always on the point of becoming frozen, ears and nose constantly dead, having to wrap up so as to become so unwieldy as to resemble the elegant movements of an elephant; besides, the roads, far from being smooth, in some places full of holes and deep ruts! Let them try this delightful journey, and I think they will never descant again so enthusiastically on the subject. I am persuaded, had any one run up against me, dressed as I was, I should have gone over, and never have been able to rise again without assistance. My costume consisted of numberless underclothes, a very thick fur coat, a huge deerskin, which always took me five minutes to get into, and then left me in a perfect state of exhaustion; three pairs of variously made stockings, and over them a huge pair of felt boots, resembling the famous seven-league boots of the fairy tale. I once wanted to cross my legs, and had to ask my friend Mr. Walcott to do it for me, which he did with some difficulty, uncrossing them again for me afterwards. A thick sort of mittens lined with fur, which make it impossible to take hold of anything; a fur cap right over my eyes, and a huge comforter over the chin and nose. In this costume I felt stifled, it is true, but had I been lighter clad I should have been frozen.

Continuing our route, up hill and down dale, through woods and forests, the thermometer 20° below zero, the sky clear, and with splendid weather, after a quick day's work, the roads being in capital order, we reached the station of Polorino Tchérémhovskaya, a long name for a small village, at 5.30 P.M., where we dined, and I think we all felt we never enjoyed a meal better. We had eaten nothing since the morning, and Siberian air intensified our appetite.

Proceeding on through the night, stopping at various stations, we reached the town of Ka-insk on the 10th at 8 A.M. It is a small town, situated on the River Kan, which we had first to cross on the ice. It is 303 versts from Nijni Udinsk. The population is about 2300 inhabitants.

We had been in a continual descent all the night —Ka-insk being situated in a valley. We passed also during that time numerous long trains of sledges laden with merchandise, which bumped up against us in a most unpleasant manner. These trains we henceforth met the whole way, and were a constant source of annoyance and delay to us. Captain ——, who spoke German with us, quite agreed to the fact that they were *verflüchter schlitten*. We must have passed, before reaching Nijni Novgorod, thousands of these sledges. We could not help thinking what a country for a railway, considering the enormous traffic. It would no doubt much upset the calculations of those interested in the Suez Canal; and it certainly is curious that Russia does not avail herself of what would be the shortest and most easy route to China.

We left Ka-insk again at 11.20 A.M., and proceeded over a very hilly country, and saw on the way, which was only thinly wooded, prints of animals' footsteps, evidently wolves.

After a drive of twenty-five versts, much annoyed by the large trains of sledges which we met, we reached Bolchiourinskaya at 1.30 P.M., and here found to our great disgust that our friend the Captain, who managed to leave something behind him at every station, having left his watch at one and purse at another, had left his *paderoshne* at Ka-insk, so we had to send back for it and wait about three hours, as we could not procure horses without it. It would be a very awkward affair for any traveller to lose his paderoshne, as it would be impossible to get on without it.

Leaving again about 4 P.M. we passed over several high hills which much impeded our progress. Here we found it necessary to increase our offers of drinking money to thirty kopecks. Our plan was always at starting to offer to the driver, according to the distance, a certain sum if he reached the next station at a given time, and although by so doing one runs the risk of a broken neck it ensures speed. The horses generally gallop away, the driver having very little power over them as there are only two outside reins, the five horses being harnessed abreast.

The animals were generally good, but not so excellent as I had heard them described. Nevertheless we sometimes travelled fifteen miles in one hour.

The roads were becoming bad as we advanced, as the commercial traffic was in full swing and the heavy sledges laden with merchandise destroyed the roads.

About a month later they become so bad as to be nearly impracticable for light sledges to pass over; they are then renewed by the various villages and towns by the use of forced labour. January is generally the coldest month in Siberia.

At one of the stations we found some tolerable Russian spirit made from corn, so we laid in a small stock. It was awfully strong, but no doubt the Siberians need it to neutralise the quantity of fat they eat.

We had to go over a very rough bit of road, which jolted us about most awfully, and very much weakened the top of our sledge.

At times, when we were going full speed we would come to a rut a foot or two deep. Bump goes the sledge, with such a force as to make every bone in one's body ache. We used to look ahead for these ruts, so as to be prepared for them. We invariably found one at the bottom of a hill. The Captain, who was talking on one occasion, not being aware of our approaching one of them, nearly bit his tongue out. I must say, looking forward to the journey we had still before us, and hearing that as we advanced the roads would become worse, Mr. Walcott and myself did heartily wish ourselves at Moscow. The Captain, whom long experience in sledge travelling in Siberia had made indifferent to the most violent bumps and dangers of being capsized, generally slept between the various post stations and did not seem at all inconvenienced. How we used to envy his capacity for sleeping!

We only arrived at Kloutchevskaya at 8.30 P.M. —distance twenty-two versts. Travelling over a better road at night, we reached, at 8 A.M., 133 versts from Bolcheourinskaya, the small station of Kouskounskaya. We were delayed during the night for one hour at one of the stations as we were all asleep, and one of us awoke to find our sledge standing in the street without horses and no one near.

Passing through Bothoyskaya, over the most execrable roads, the snow having drifted, the roads being much exposed to the wind, which was blowing rather too strong to be pleasant, we reached Krasnoyarsk, having gone some eight versts on the River Yenisee which was entirely frozen, and over which our little horses took us at tremendous speed. The distance from Irkoutsk is 1006 versts, one quarter of the way to Nijni Novgorod. The Yenisee is a magnificent river, about 3000 miles long — I believe the longest known river in the world. It rises somewhere near the Taugnon Mountains, not very far from Kiachta, and falls into the Frozen Ocean.

The town of Krasnoyarsk, though small, is very clean and well-built, and has some handsome buildings in it; it is most beautifully situated in the Yenisee province, the governor of which resides there. The meaning of the word Krasnoyarsk is, " well-situated "—a most appropriate name for the town. We had a good dinner there, and replenished our stores; it was a welcome break in our journey, and gave us new vigour to proceed.

However, we did not delay long there, as although we should have much liked to have passed a night out of our sledge, still we wanted more to get on as fast as possible, so we left again at 4 P.M. We had our sledge, which sadly needed it, repaired.

We reached Kalokemzongskaya — fifty-seven versts from the last town—at 9 P.M., and then went steadily on to Atchinsk—108 versts further on, which place we reached at 9 A.M. of the 12th, having made the last twelve miles in fifty minutes.

Atchinsk is the last town in Eastern Siberia. It

is only a small place, and famous for nothing that I could find out except a very capital post station, where we made a good breakfast.

We only stayed there for half an hour, and jogged on again over better roads to Bogotolskaya, making the last thirty versts in one hour and twenty-five minutes—truly a tremendous pace!

We here learnt, by an incident that happened on the way, that there are other privileges attached to the two-stamp pass than those I have already enumerated.

A sledge was ahead of us with merchants in it, who of course only had one stamp; our driver called upon them to let us pass, which they were obliged to do, and they were not able to pass us again even if their horses were faster. Of course by this means we always secured the best horses at the various stations.

During the whole day we made good progress, arriving at Thraginskaya, 247 versts from Krasnoyarsk, at 4 P.M. On the 13th we made Berikoubskaya, at 7 A.M., after a good night's journey, and at nine o'clock we reached Potehitanskaya, having made 130 versts since nine last evening. It was bitterly cold, colder than we had ever felt it, and I think we all, including the Captain, felt thoroughly miserable and done up, and longed for the end of the journey.

Our sledge on one occasion nearly tipped over, which did not add to our happiness. In the complaint-book, which one finds at all the stations, I found the following complaint recorded at the last-named station :

" A traveller having finished his tea, and having halted for half an hour, found, on going outside to see why he was so long delayed, that his old horses were still unharnessed. In a great rage he approached the coachman and demanded the reason. 'Don't put yourself in a fuss,' said the Tartar Jehu, ' you only cut a small figure in the world, so you can afford to wait.' "

No doubt the complaining traveller had given a very small drink-money, and suffered for his ill-placed economy accordingly.

A very smooth road through dense woods again brought us to Koljanskaya, and there we actually found the postmaster was going to feed— an operation we thought they never performed as we had never caught them at it—and, for a consideration, we shared some remarkably large and greasy *cotelettes*, which were like manna in the desert to us. A peculiar sort of cucumber, soaked in lamp-oil, we could not stomach; we did take a small piece to try, and the effects nearly left us as empty as we were before. Our friend the Captain, and host, the postmaster, thought us very squeamish, and devoured a double share accordingly.

Passing over a very bad road for some way, and then over a better one, we made a rapid run, and reached the town of Tomsk in the evening of the 13th.

Tomsk is 1561 versts from Irkoutsk. We felt glad to get there, and we put up at the only hotel in the place, and a most miserable one it was. It was a long time before we could even get any food. They had no bill of fare, like an ordinary hotel, and no wine, so we had to send out for some, which, as it was late, we procured with some difficulty, and after a great deal of trouble we induced the owner of the hotel, who seemed perfectly indifferent to our being there or not, to get us some of the inevitable cutlets.

The hotel was a barrack of a place, with no sort of regulation or cleanliness. The attendance consisted of two very dirty housemaids. The company, who were playing cards in an adjoining room to where we were, taking what supper they could get, certainly did not seem select. One enormously fat old woman seemed to be the greatest authority amongst them. To call such a slovenly establishment a hotel certainly was paying it a compliment; however we were all glad to turn in afterwards into a small room, in which there were three sofas, and, well covered with wraps, we got a good sound sleep until the morning, which we much needed.

Finding that there were no post-horses available we had to hire private ones, for which of course we had to pay three times as much, and then, when we were ready, we discovered that our sledge was broken and wanted repairing.

I forgot to mention that at Atchinsk we had sold our old sledge for five roubles, as it had become nothing but a bundle of ropes and bits of wood and we expected to see it tumble to pieces, and had purchased a very good new one for thirty roubles. However, it was a bad turn-out, wanting repairs already; but it is a wonder how any sledges last at all, considering the roads they have to pass over. While the sledge is repairing I will give a few words regarding Tomsk.

It is considered one of the coldest towns in Siberia. Whilst we were there it was tremendous; a strong wind blowing, no sun, and a regular black cold, the thermometer showing 70° to 80° of frost. Hardly any one could be seen in the streets, the inhabitants seldom venturing out.

It certainly is not an interesting town, and in the winter it is full of gold-diggers out of employ, who do not add to its respectability.

It is a large commercial town, containing about 20,000 inhabitants, including 300 Poles. It is a transit town, and also a free town. It is situated on the river Tom, a branch of the river Ob, which rises in the Allatan Mountains and flows into the Frozen Ocean. We got some new felt boots there and laid in a supply of wine, &c.

At 2.30 P.M., repairs being completed and having rearranged our sledge, which was more comfortable accordingly, we started off again, and made Proscacova, seventy-three versts, at 6.30 P.M. The first forty versts the road were very bad, but the latter portion made up for it, being in splendid order, and we sped along over its smooth surface at fully fifteen miles per hour. The country there changes very much and becomes flat and uninteresting, and very few trees—a sign that we were approaching the steppe of Baraba, which is nearly as much a desert as that of Gobi, only more inhabited and fertile.

We reached the small town of Kolyvrane on the 15th, at 9 P.M.; 216 versts, since 12 A.M. yesterday. It is only a small town, of no importance, containing about 2000 inhabitants. The roads were all good, and the cold was not so intense as it had been. I think if it had lasted we should have had some difficulty in existing, for, without any exaggeration, we were very nearly frozen.

A very curious outbreak occurred amongst the peasantry situated in some of the villages near Kolyvrane a short time before we passed through it. A man who professed to have written authority from the Emperor came and told them that a special decree had been passed in their favour, excusing them from ever paying any more taxes. As the peasantry are entirely ignorant of the accomplishments of reading and writing they rejoiced excessively and fully believed him.

When the government tax-gatherer came among them and demanded the usual taxes they all refused, saying that the Emperor had let them off. It was useless to remonstrate and try to prove the absurdity of the thing.

The governor of Tomsk then sent to them, but as they believed he only wanted the taxes for his own use, the Emperor having freed them from paying them, they broke out into open rebellion. Troops were sent and had to shoot some of these unfortunate deluded peasantry, and quiet was again restored. Whether the author of the whole disturbance was caught I did not hear. I hope he was, and well punished.

I could not help thinking of the agitations and strikes that have occurred in England, generally brought on in a similar manner by the visit of some scheming villain who has nothing to lose, intruding his hypocritical presence among a body of men who, until he had whispered his lies among them, never dreamt that they were not happy before, and as well off as they ought to be.

We cannot condemn the poor ignorant peasantry of Siberia for being so easily deluded, when Englishmen allow themselves to be influenced by the leading of some knave or other who has no interest in their welfare, but only works for his own ends.

We had long been looking forward to the steppe of Baraba, dreaded by every traveller in the winter months—everywhere we had passed through the horrors of the steppes had been impressed upon us—and it was with no pleasant impressions that we at last entered its precincts, two stations from Kolyvrane, at a place called Krouthialoga.

Our happiness certainly was not enhanced by the fact of a tremendously bitter north-east wind blowing, driving clouds of snow before it, and so dense as nearly to render it impossible to proceed.

One must visit the Baraba to see a similar snowstorm. The natives call such a tempest a *borum*, and it sometimes lasts for a week at a time. How dismal we felt, and how we shivered, chilled to the very bone! The only redeeming point was that the horses, being nearly wild, took us at a tremendous pace. Although I must say, from all I had heard of the magnificence of the Tartar horses found on the steppes, I was very much disappointed.

As we proceeded the trees became very scarce, and we could nearly fancy ourselves back again in the great desert of Gobi. The snow, which was falling thicker and thicker and rendering us more and more miserable, made the roads so heavy that it became difficult for our five half-wild horses to lug the sledge through the heavy drifts.

There are no natural methods of showing the whereabouts of the roads, so the natives have resorted to a very ingenious method. They place at intervals at each side of the road small stacks of straw, which catch the snow and form small hills, which serve as marks to indicate the route. Without this it would be the easiest possible thing to be lost on the steppe, and from all I saw, the unfortunate occupants of a sledge, who, caught in one of these snow-storms, wandered from the route, most probably would not be heard of again before summer heat should dissolve the snow and expose their remains to view.

Although we did feel excessively gloomy still we had one consolation, and that was, that every verst took one off the 900 or more that we had to accomplish before leaving the steppe.

After a great deal of floundering about and vast exertion on the part of our quadrupeds, we arrived at Kolmacova on the 15th. Here we were informed that by taking another route, and avoiding Tumen, we could shorten our journey by 300 versts, which of course was most gratifying intelligence to us; but we afterwards found out it was all a dodge to get us out of the government road, so that we should be forced to take private posthorses, which with few exceptions were not as good as those we always obtained at the government post stations. However, we swallowed the bait, and exceedingly repented of having done so later on. For all the peasants' houses we stopped at whilst horses were changed were disgusting and dirty, and every dodge was resorted to to delay us and fleece us, and we felt quite helpless under the process.

At one place we stopped at we were entertained by perhaps the most villainous-looking family that a man might wish to see. I shall never forget the paterfamilias of the establishment, who told us he was a discharged soldier, and attempted to be amiable, in a cut-throat sort of manner, grinning most diabolically all the time; his attempts at familiarity, as far as we were concerned, were a failure. I could not help shuddering at the thought, what a poor chance we should have stood if travelling singly, and I could not help wondering how many dead bodies of unfortunate travellers were buried in his garden. The whole place looked like murder. It was the only time during our journey that I think we really did feel a sense of real fear; but we took good care not to show it.

When we left, our cut-throat looking host presented us with a small account for a few potatoes he had supplied us with, his wife, who looked as bad as himself, quietly working, one could have imagined, at our shrouds. Of course it was exorbitant, but what could we do but pay it?—as the whole village I have no doubt would have gone against us, and I am sure we felt glad to be off at any price.

Never did the open air feel so fresh and welcome to me as it did then, after the stinking close room we had left, and its occupants. After this adventure we decided to regain the government roads as soon as we could, although they might be longer.

As I have before stated, we were deceived entirely about them; I think the whole difference was about forty or fifty versts. The villages all through the steppe look poor, and the natives certainly are not prepossessing. They do not compare with those of Eastern Siberia. From what I saw I think it was a matter of congratulation to get across it without mishap.

CHAPTER XI.

A Collision with another Sledge—The Country of Windmills—The Telegraph Wires broken by the Snow—Disgusting Condition of the Peasant Post-houses—Wolves—The River Irtish—We quit the Steppe of Baraba—Abstemiousness and Trustworthiness of Russian Drivers—Besroucova—Our Driver nearly takes us over a Bank—Our Russian Fellow-traveller leaves everything behind him—A splendid Sunset—The Country begins to improve—A Sable in view—We reach the Top of the Pass of the Oural Mountains—The plain white Stone that marks the Separation between Asia and Europe—We arrive at Nijni Novgorod, and bid farewell to our Sledges, and proceed by Rail to Moscow, and thence on to St. Petersburg.

AT five o'clock on the 16th we reached the town of Khainsk, a small and uninteresting place, so we got on at once, and thank goodness the fury of the borum was exhausted and it was not half so cold. The roads were in good order, the fresh snow being already quite hard. We were going at full speed, when crash, bump, we smashed into a cart. Away went the door of our sledge and a good part of the top, and for a moment we thought the whole top part was going. We did not, however, wait to ascertain the extent of the damage done, for the very simple reason that our steeds would not stop, their method being to pull up only at the next station.

During the last twenty-four hours we had made 250 versts, nearly ten miles an hour, which we considered rather good travelling, and considering stopping to change horses every hour and a half, could hardly have been excelled.

The desert there becomes very barren and thinly inhabited. What a country it would have been for Don Quixote!—for anything like the quantity of windmills I never saw before. Every village possesses two or three, and such antiquated arrangements can scarcely be imagined. In one village, or rather outside it, we counted thirty-three windmills, all in a row. Whatever they could be wanted for I cannot conceive.

I remember that village so well because we started from it early in the morning and somehow or other, by the extraordinary way the road is marked out, we seemed to be continually finding ourselves either on the north, south, east, or west side of these thirty-three windmills. We tried to account for the phenomenon, but as we could not we gave it up.

A most extraordinary feature that we noticed

all through Siberia was, that the telegraph posts from Kiachta to Russia Proper were planted in the most extraordinary places, generally extending over five miles where three would have been enough. Whether this was a job on the part of the contractor, which I shrewdly suspect, or there were reasons too deep for us to fathom, we certainly could not but feel mystified and full of wonder.

One thing certainly did impress us as being excessively useful : every post had its number and date—a necessary precaution, as they have to be renewed after the damage caused to them by the furious storms which occur. No wonder telegraphic communication sometimes is interrupted in the winter; for when we passed the wires were literally bent to the earth by the weight of frozen snow upon them, and in many places had given way. I should think that small stations at intervals, during the winter months, with a couple of men in each to look after the wires, would well repay the trouble.

I know we reported a broken wire at one of the post stations, and we were told that as they had no communication at the station we had better let it be known at a town some 200 versts farther on. No doubt telegrams suffered delay accordingly.

We reached Kamichova at 7 A.M. on the 17th. (I may here mention that the sun rose at 10 and set at 1.30.) This is sometimes called the commencement of the Baraba; but why I do not know, as there are no distinctive features to justify it.

Here we struck into what is called the New Route, and for the time the crown posts also end, so that we were driven to use the private posts, which however are tolerably well organised by a company under a crown charter.

We breakfasted at Kamichova, at a peasant's hut, and although I was very hungry when we arrived there my appetite entirely forsook me, for we had to pass through a room where the whole family, male and female, were sleeping. There was no ventilation of any sort, and a huge stove, sending volumes of dry heat forth, created a most unpleasant atmosphere although it was intensely cold. Mr. Walcott and myself made a precipitate escape into the open air again, and remained in our sledge until we departed, satisfying ourselves with a few biscuits. Our Russian friend however enjoyed his breakfast—I suppose being inured to that sort of thing—and laughed at us considerably for our squeamishness. Certainly it may be imagined, after the inconveniences we had put up with during the whole journey, that we would have become accustomed to such trifles; but I am sorry to say we never were able, with any degree of comfort or pleasure, to enter a peasant's house or post station in Siberia, for the reasons mentioned above.

In four hours after leaving the last station, over a good road, the distance being fifty-six versts, we reached Raisino.

All the villages we passed through at this stage of our journey were fenced round with strong wooden palisades, there being a gate at each end. The reason for this we never learnt. They may have been constructed to keep out the wolves in winter.

We were entertained at the various places we stopped at with the most dismal prints of travellers being attacked, devoured, and hard beset by wolves. We always inquired if these animals had become troublesome, and were glad to be told that their larders had not yet required to be replenished, although there were plenty on the road; of which fact we had good proof, as we saw plenty of them, and good large animals they were.

Fifty-nine versts farther on we reached Poustinskaya, near the banks of the great river Irtish.

It is famous among the natives for an event which took place in the year 1600.

Yermac, a celebrated Cossack chief, renowned for his mighty deeds and prowess in battle, with a few followers, had overrun Siberia, and taken from the Mongol Emperor Camuc a large portion of his territory in these parts. Camuc, who had collected the whole flower of his army, and had vainly pursued Yermac, at last came upon him at this village, having an overwhelming force at his disposal. After a severe battle, Yermac's army, consisting only of some 400 to 500 Cossacks, was defeated. Seeing all was lost, Yermac, with only two followers, rode furiously down the steep banks of the Irtish, and attempted to cross its rapidly flowing waters, but, being clad in armour, they were drowned; and thus perished one of the greatest warrior bandits of the time. This was the anecdote told us, but I cannot vouch for its authenticity.

The Irtish is the second longest river in Siberia. It rises in Tartary, and flows into the Frozen Ocean. It is a curious thing, finding this river there, as it divides two flat plains, the one we left being much higher than the plain on the other side. We had to descend a very steep bank, I should think

200 or 300 feet, before we reached the frozen river.

From lack of all indications we should never have guessed that a large river was before us, so sudden was our approach to it and so unexpected.

On the opposite side, some eighteen versts from the last station, is situated a village or small town called Mogilnaya, meaning "burial-place." It was there that Yermac first encountered Camuc, some time before his final defeat, and routed him with great slaughter.

At 2.30 A.M., on the 18th, eighty-one versts from Mogilnaya, we reached Angala. The thermometer being only as low as zero, 32° of frost, with all our wraps, &c., we felt unpleasantly warm.

The country here, although still flat, begins to show indications of quitting the desert or steppe of Baraba. We could distinguish on our right-hand side a ridge of cliffs and a few trees here and there. The villages also became more plentiful, but very poor, and we were bothered with beggars, the first we had seen in Siberia. Although this was unpleasant it told us we were approaching nearer to Russia Proper. Passing several stations we reached Thoukalinsk, a small town where the steppes may be said to finish, and much to our delight. Before leaving the steppe of Baraba I must contradict a fiction which all travellers seem to have imbibed, or perhaps imagined, respecting it. We had heard that all the horses in the Baraba were wild, in fact required four or five men to hold them at each station; that immediately they were released they started off at full gallop, going some eighteen miles an hour; that nothing would stop them until they arrived at the next station.

I used to feel rather a dread of these wild horses of the Baraba before I saw them, imagining all manner of upsets, &c., but I found it was only a fiction, as we certainly travelled through the Baraba slower than in any other part. We used to annoy our kind Russian friend very much by asking when we were to meet these fiery steeds, as he was also much imbued with the idea of their existing somewhere about. Of course at times we did meet with half-wild animals, but seldom whilst traversing the Baraba.

We avoided Omsk, thus shortening our journey, according to native account, by sixty-four versts, and by our own reckoning by only thirty-nine versts. The natives are, I should say, profoundly ignorant of reckoning distances, as even at the post stations they were often wrong.

About five miles before reaching Thoukalinsk we entered the government post roads again, and although they were in a very rough condition we were glad, as the peasant posts are not good, and are not so rapid in changing horses. I would strongly advise the traveller to stick to the ordinary post routes, although the distance may be longer, as I do not believe it takes more time.

At this small town we noticed that some of the houses were made of brick—the first we had seen in Siberia.

Another fiction we had been told before starting, and indeed had read in books, was that we should find all the yemschiks, or drivers, drunkards. I can affirm that we found them all most abstemious, civil, and obliging. I do not remember ever finding one of our drivers drunk, or approaching to it. For civility and sobriety they set a bright example to the drivers of the four-wheeled cabs in the civilised city of London.

When I make the above statement I do so on the fact that we had at various times 180 different drivers, whilst on our journey through Siberia, and 900 horses.

Our route now took us to Krouthaya, a small village forty-eight versts from Thoukalinsk. We proceeded at a rapid pace, passing several stations and changing at each one as usual; the road being very smooth and slanting our sledge insisted upon going forward sideways, which was pleasant as a change, but rather dangerous. At Khamichenna, where we intended getting something to eat, we were disappointed, as the post people could give us none, and we were out of provisions ourselves. After leaving we crossed the River Ichim, which flows into the Irtish that side of Abatsky. Bowling along at a tremendous pace, at times on the point of capsizing, a bright moon shining as clear as daylight, the thermometer a few degrees below zero, passing through several villages, very poor in appearance but mostly built of brick, we made Besroucova at 6 A.M. on the 19th, and precious glad we were to arrive, as we had eaten nothing since the morning before, and the pace we had been driving over ruts and hillocks had nearly broken our bones. Our Russian friend however seemed to like it.

Once during the night one of our drivers, going at a tremendous pace, as near as possible took us over a bank, and we should most decidedly have been killed, as we could see a yawning chasm ready to receive us. I certainly would not advise a nervous individual to go sledging in Siberia, as it really places the traveller in a constant state of excitement. I used to wonder how our sledge could stand it—the fearful jolts it sometimes got and communicated to us. I must say I did now and then heartily wish myself at the end of the journey, as I scarcely expected to arrive at its conclusion without some mishap. The roads get very bad at that period of the year, and at times heavy falls of snow render them perfectly impassable.

We managed at a peasant's house to get some breakfast, and there our Russian friend discovered that he had left his purse and watch at one of the stations where we had changed horses during the night. I verily believe when we reached Moscow he had left everything he had at different stations. A memorandum book of mine, his own military cap, which he would insist upon wearing at times until the cold made him change to his fur cap again, pencil-case, knives—all managed to slip through his fingers. We always used to ask him if he had left anything behind him, when we were not asleep.

I shall never forget a sunset we saw in the afternoon. People who have never seen such a one cannot imagine it. A painter, if he could paint such a picture, would not be believed. The ground, covered with snow, gradually becoming blood red; the sun sinking behind a mass of clouds, which lightened up into most wonderful colours and forms; in the horizon a clear space which looked like a bright and glorious city, such as we could imagine heaven to be. Even our stolid Russian friend was enthusiastic, as minarets, towers, gates, distinctly came into view, and dying out, gave place to other shapes. It certainly was a glimpse into eternity, and a vague yearning came over me to be there and find that rest which is not attained here on earth.

As we proceeded we were much annoyed by beggars, and the villages became poorer, and afforded no signs of prosperity—a great contrast to Eastern Siberia. But the country improves in appearance and loses its desert-like air; it is less flat and is thickly wooded, and affords good cover for animals of prey. We saw several pure white pheasants and some very splendidly plumaged jays. Birch trees are decidedly more plentiful than others, though farther on pines take their place. We continued to pass long transports laden with merchandise, and the continual bumps we encountered neither improved our sledge nor our tempers.

When we reached Vagayskaya we found out that at the last station we had not been to the regular post station, our driver having told us a lie and taken us to a peasant's house—and a villainous place it was, as well as its owner. This is a regular dodge, and we only discovered it when we were driven into a peasant's place again, and we insisted upon being at once taken to the proper post station, and made no end of a row, which resulted in the yemschik being flogged and the peasant fined.

We reached Tumen on the 20th, $493\frac{3}{4}$ versts from Thoucalinsk. It is a small and flourishing town, but as we were anxious now to get on we made no stay, and proceeded with all speed to Ekaterinburg, named after the Empress Catherine, which place we reached on the 21st. Ekaterinburg is a fine town, and well worth seeing. It contains some handsome buildings in stone, but it was too cold for us to do much and we were anxious to proceed, as we knew several generals, &c., were not far behind us, and would monopolise our horses if we gave them the start. They never did catch us, as although they were supposed to be travelling with all speed we must have been travelling with more than all speed, as we gradually shook them off. We left at 12 A.M. on the 22nd, and had to take post sledges, sending ours on in advance, the roads being very bad. I never went over such remarkable roads, through forests, over ditches, bumping away against the trees. I saw a sable—such a funny little animal, something like a ferret. I believe it is the most ferocious little animal known. It will fight to the death with its own species, or if caught or attacked will bite through leg, arm, or anything it can lay hold of.

We had been gradually ascending the Oural mountains, but it was so imperceptibly that we hardly knew it. The pass across the Ourals extends over 180 miles, so that the ascent would necessarily be very gradual. At 4 P.M. we reached the summit of the pass, and there we saw the plain white stone, with Asia engraved on one side and Europe on the other, which marks the frontier, and happy did we feel to find ourselves at last again in Europe.

We had intended celebrating the event by drinking a bottle of champagne reserved for the occasion, but as it was frozen to the very bottom we were unable to do so. At 5.30 P.M. we reached Thatiza, the first village in Europe, and here we again took our own sledge and made good way up to Perm, 364¼ versts from Ekatarinburg. At Perm we laid in a stock of malachite and other curiosities, which are very cheap indeed at that town. We only paid about a fifth of what we were asked for similar things in Moscow. From Perm we took a billet which carried us on to the next town, where it had to be renewed, and saves the trouble of paying at each post station.

The scenery becomes very tame. The villages large and poor, and the posting very bad; in fact that part of the journey is the worst, and of course is felt more, as, the end of the journey being near, every delay and annoyance seem to crop up in order to prolong it. The cold was awful—40° below zero—and our feet and hands suffered very much. How intensely we longed to get to Nijni Novgorod!

At Perm we were photographed in our sledge, and at the same time nearly frozen. A large quantity of government gold was telegraphed as coming, so, luckily, we were requested to herald it on the way, and order at each station sixty horses, which procured us a *gold pass*, ordering all post masters to forward us with all expedition—a stroke of luck as unexpected as it was welcome.

On the 29th we reached Kazan, celebrated for its soap and leather and also for being a very handsome little town; and on the 30th, at 4 P.M., we arrived at Nijni Novgorod, and bade farewell to our sledge. We had some difficulty in finding a hotel, as all were full, but at last we found one by the celebrated market-place where the fair is held, and I cannot say much for its accommodation. The Volga was frozen over, and the cold intense. Two days were enough, so we proceeded by rail to Moscow—very comfortable after the sledge, but not much faster. At Moscow we tarried for three days and then on to St. Petersburg—and there ends my journey. I did not regret having done it, as it was over; but I do not think anything would tempt me to follow the same route again. Once in a lifetime is more than sufficient.

As I read over the pages I have written I feel they are woefully deficient as regards describing the events, experiences, and hardships we underwent. I have, however, done my best. I can only wish that any of my readers could have been with us—in spirit, not bodily, as I have no evil wish against him or her—and I do really think then they would agree that a journey from China to St. Petersburg in the winter months is a memorable undertaking worth relating. *Jam satis.*

www.ingramcontent.com/pod-product-compliance
Lightning Source LLC
Chambersburg PA
CBHW030303240426
43673CB00040B/1040